"Many contemporary analyses o
looking view of the power dynamic
with their flock. These analyses the
prevention of clergy ethics violation
points beyond a rules-based model
deeply rooted Christian spiritual di,

moral health. These practices, Wheeler argues, are the tools that will most fruitfully shield churches and their clergy from ethics abuse and will build abundant communities of faith. *Sustaining Ministry*, along with Wheeler's earlier *The Minister as Moral Theologian*, is a must-read for everyone in ministry, from bishops to lay pastors."

—**Kathryn Greene-McCreight**, author of Darkness Is My Only Companion: A Christian Response to Mental Illness

"Wheeler draws on her deep familiarity with what makes ministry distinct as a profession and a way of life. She writes beautifully and accessibly; often I felt I was as much listening to her wise counsel as reading it. She skillfully weaves insights from clergy self-care with pastoral ethics, and while she is unflinchingly realistic about the moral dangers of ministry, she is also sympathetic toward those who try to navigate them. This book will be especially useful in seminary contexts and for those just entering the ministry profession."

—**Barbara J. Blodgett**, author of Lives Entrusted: An Ethic of Trust for Ministry

"This new book by Sondra Wheeler provides a wealth of practical wisdom for readers. While policies, procedures, and professional codes of ethics are important, Professor Wheeler reminds us they cannot do all the work of moral and ministerial formation. Through this book, we are called to develop deeper reservoirs for sustaining ministry through practices of prayer and accountability. These practices help ministers and Christian leaders live into the goodness of God so that they in turn are better able to help churches and communities grow in God's goodness and to faithfully extend that goodness outward to the world. I will be using this book in my classes."

—**Wyndy Corbin Reuschling**, Ashland Theological Seminary

"Sondra Wheeler combines ethical, biblical, and theological expertise with thorough analytical skills to address dilemmas of clergy life. Drawing on the serving heritage of professions, she shows how clergy face special issues, particularly around power. She performs a careful diagnosis of perils and temptations clergy encounter while offering positive practices to sustain an ethical ministry."

—**Lovett H. Weems Jr.**, Wesley Theological Seminary

SUSTAINING MINISTRY

SUSTAINING MINISTRY

FOUNDATIONS AND PRACTICES
for SERVING FAITHFULLY

SONDRA WHEELER

Baker Academic
a division of Baker Publishing Group
Grand Rapids, Michigan

© 2017 by Sondra Ely Wheeler

Published by Baker Academic
a division of Baker Publishing Group
PO Box 6287, Grand Rapids, MI 49516-6287
www.bakeracademic.com

Printed in the United States of America

Library of Congress Cataloging-in-Publication Data
Names: Wheeler, Sondra Ely, 1956– author.
Title: Sustaining ministry : foundations and practices for serving faithfully / Sondra Wheeler.
Description: Grand Rapids : Baker Academic, 2017. | Includes index.
Identifiers: LCCN 2017020097 | ISBN 9780801098369 (pbk. : alk. paper)
Subjects: LCSH: Clergy—Professional ethics. | Clergy—Conduct of life. | Pastoral theology. | Character.
Classification: LCC BV4011.5 .W444 2017 | DDC 241/.641—dc23
LC record available at https://lccn.loc.gov/2017020097

17 18 19 20 21 22 23   7 6 5 4 3 2 1

To all the pastors who have shared with me
their successes and failures in ministry,
whose hard-earned insights made this work possible

Contents

Acknowledgments

This book is largely the fruit of conversations conducted over more than twenty years with long-serving ministers and new student-pastors, district superintendents and bishops, and judicatory officials from several denominations. Occasionally they involved congregants whose pastors had gotten into moral difficulties of one kind or another. It would be impossible, and probably unwise, to name all these interlocutors. Those who have participated in these conversations may recognize themselves in this book, but I would not be surprised if they did not. (We often do not realize the impact our casual remarks may have on someone else.) In any case, I remember them and remain grateful for their particular insights and contributions.

Special thanks are owed to Reverend Anna Copeland, pastor in the United Church of Christ, who read and responded to some of the most delicate sections of the text, sharing with me the fruit of her considerable experience and challenging me to rethink some of my own judgments. The Reverend Peter Moon, district superintendent in the United Methodist Church, patiently entertained my questions and offered me his own perspective on questions of policy and procedure in cases of misconduct, which was very helpful.

I also garnered ideas and insights from others in the field of ministerial ethics, several of whom are cited in the text or whose work is included in the list of further readings. But even among colleagues, it was often the collateral discussions at meetings and the exchange of stories we had heard or been part of that proved most provocative and useful. In this regard I think especially of Joe Kotva, a colleague with many years of pastoral experience, and Rebekah Miles, professor of Christian Ethics at SMU. In exchanges with such people I discovered illuminating patterns, consistent ways in which ministers begin to go wrong, and likewise consistent ways they find their way back in time (or don't).

There is, I have learned, no formula—no policy or procedure or set of rules that can guarantee that a person will not become confused or cynical about the role of pastor and misuse its powers. But there are ways forward, strategies and disciplines that help ministers negotiate the challenges they face and offer them safe and healthy ways to receive the support every human being needs. What I know about these practices I have learned chiefly from listening to and watching others, gifted pastors like the Reverend Daniel Mejia and the Reverend Dr. Scott Kisker who have long been sustained by them. I am grateful for their example as well as their instruction. Finally, I remain grateful to all the ministers I have had the privilege of working with as students, teachers, and colleagues over many years. Their faces, voices, and stories crowd my imagination, and it is to them I have dedicated this work.

Abbreviations

Old Testament

Gen.	Genesis	Song of Sol.	Song of Solomon
Exod.	Exodus	Isa.	Isaiah
Lev.	Leviticus	Jer.	Jeremiah
Num.	Numbers	Lam.	Lamentations
Deut.	Deuteronomy	Ezek.	Ezekiel
Josh.	Joshua	Dan.	Daniel
Judg.	Judges	Hosea	Hosea
Ruth	Ruth	Joel	Joel
1–2 Sam.	1–2 Samuel	Amos	Amos
1–2 Kings	1–2 Kings	Obad.	Obadiah
1–2 Chron.	1–2 Chronicles	Jon.	Jonah
Ezra	Ezra	Mic.	Micah
Neh.	Nehemiah	Nah.	Nahum
Esther	Esther	Hab.	Habakkuk
Job	Job	Zeph.	Zephaniah
Ps. (Pss.)	Psalms	Hag.	Haggai
Prov.	Proverbs	Zech.	Zechariah
Eccles.	Ecclesiastes	Mal.	Malachi

New Testament

Matt.	Matthew	John	John
Mark	Mark	Acts	Acts
Luke	Luke	Rom.	Romans

1–2 Cor.	1–2 Corinthians	Philem.	Philemon
Gal.	Galatians	Heb.	Hebrews
Eph.	Ephesians	James	James
Phil.	Philippians	1–2 Pet.	1–2 Peter
Col.	Colossians	1–3 John	1–3 John
1–2 Thess.	1–2 Thessalonians	Jude	Jude
1–2 Tim.	1–2 Timothy	Rev.	Revelation
Titus	Titus		

Introduction

Why Good Rules Aren't Enough

This book is one of a pair of companion volumes that address different aspects of the relationship between ethics and ministry. The other volume focuses on the elements of pastoral leadership that call on a minister to serve as resident moral theologian for her or his community.[1] These include preaching on biblical passages that are ethically demanding, confusing, or even offensive, as well as teaching about ethical issues that are controversial or divisive within the church. They also include offering counsel to those facing moral uncertainty or temptation. Finally, there is the fact of being taken as a model of discipleship—a feature of the minister's role that many find problematic but that cannot be avoided. These dimensions of ministry are essential for the church to preserve its identity as a moral community: a place of moral reflection and conversation, a context of mutual support but also of mutual accountability. Such tasks require ministers to possess knowledge and a particular set of skills, which are treated at length in the companion volume.

But as the necessity of serving as a model of faithful life makes clear, more is needed to lead a moral community than information

1. Sondra Wheeler, *The Minister as Moral Theologian: Ethical Dimensions of Pastoral Leadership* (Grand Rapids: Baker Academic, 2017).

and techniques. To fulfill these obligations also requires that a minister become a certain kind of person. Moreover, she or he must sustain the required character through the distinctive challenges and risks that come with intimate engagement in the moral and spiritual lives of others. The present book is about these challenges—why they run so deep in ministry, why they can be so difficult to negotiate success-fully, and how one might prepare to navigate them across the decades of a life devoted to pastoral leadership.

Insofar as this is a book about the ethical demands of ministry, it is hardly alone. In the last twenty-five years several works have been published in this area, some general and others focused on special topics such as sexual misconduct.[2] I have found many of these volumes useful in my decades of teaching about the ethics of ministry. All of them offer clear expositions of the shape and seriousness of pastoral obligations, and of the potentially devastating consequences when those obligations are not met. They lay out helpful rules to protect congregants or counselees from abuse and harm by those entrusted with caring for them. Several of them provide useful practical guid-ance and sound advice for ministers, which aim at avoiding confusion and miscommunication about their role and help them to establish barriers that prevent accidental violations of professional norms. Taken together, these books represent a great advance in the clarity and concreteness of preparation for pastoral work as they are read in seminary courses and contexts of continuing education.

What one does not regularly find in these texts, however, is insight into how and why even ministers who set out with the best inten-tions get into moral trouble—for most ministers do set out with

2. For instance, Richard John Neuhaus, *Freedom for Ministry*, 2nd ed. (Grand Rapids: Eerdmans, 1992); Richard M. Gula, *Ethics in Pastoral Ministry* (New York: Paulist Press, 1996); William H. Willimon, *Calling and Character: Virtues of the Ordained Life* (Nashville: Abingdon, 2000); Joe E. Trull and James E. Carter, *Min-isterial Ethics: Moral Formation for Church Leaders*, 2nd ed. (Grand Rapids: Baker Academic, 2004); Joseph E. Bush, *Gentle Shepherding: Pastoral Ethics and Leadership* (St. Louis: Chalice, 2008); Barbara Blodgett, *Lives Entrusted: An Ethic of Trust for Ministry* (Minneapolis: Fortress, 2008); Richard M. Gula, *Just Ministry: Professional Ethics for Pastoral Ministers* (New York: Paulist Press, 2010); Marie M. Fortune, *Is Nothing Sacred? When Sex Invades the Pastoral Relationship* (San Francisco: HarperSanFrancisco, 1989); Stanley J. Grenz and Roy D. Bell, *Betrayal of Trust: Confronting and Preventing Clergy Sexual Misconduct*, 2nd ed. (Grand Rapids: Baker Books, 2001).

good intentions. Predators and frauds exist in ministry as in all other fields, but they are the exception and not the rule. Thus it comes as a surprise that clergy are, for instance, statistically more likely to be guilty of violating sexual boundaries than other professionals.[3] The root of such failures has not been deeply explored in the literature. Neither is much attention paid to the peculiar demands of pastoral service or to the particular moral challenges and perils that attend that service, even (or perhaps especially) for those whose personal investment in ministry is greatest and most sincere. The work of ministry is difficult, not only practically but also morally, and has risks built into it that cannot wholly be foreclosed. Therefore, it is not enough to explain the general moral obligations of ministers, the rules that specify these obligations, or the reasons that they apply. Nor does it suffice to discuss policies and procedures for responding to ethical violations by pastors when they occur. While addressing these matters is necessary, long experience and observation have persuaded me that it is not sufficient.

Accordingly, this book focuses on the underlying dynamics that make ministry potentially dangerous both to those who practice it and to those for whom they care. To explore this, I treat matters rarely discussed in relation to pastoral ethics, like subtle distortions in the practice of ministry that signal that something has gone awry long before the financial and sexual scandals that attract media attention. The list of such distortions is long. They include an inability to delegate and an unwillingness to share authority. They may appear as a reluctance to develop leadership competence in others and a tendency to structure the church's life and worship so that the minister remains the center of attention. They may also include carelessness about elements of the minister's role that really are distinctive, such as the symbolic power of the office and the special duties of those who are entrusted with the personal confidences of congregants. Alongside

---

3. In her book, *The Cry of Tamar: Violence against Women and the Church's Response* (Minneapolis: Fortress, 1995), Pamela Cooper-White offers the following broad but reasonable estimate: "Somewhere between one in eight and one in three clergy have crossed sexual boundaries with their parishioners" (149). For comparison, a review of several self-report surveys of US physicians yields a figure of just under 7 percent reporting sexual contact with present patients. See Randy Sansone and Lori Sansone, "Crossing the Line: Sexual Boundary Violations by Physicians," *Psychiatry* 6, no. 6 (June 2009): 45–48.

these deformations of leadership, I also describe how common patterns of life among clergy may contribute to the corrosion of pastoral identity and, conversely, the ways in which the ordinary disciplines of Christian life—including the crucial discipline of rest—can undergird and protect that identity.

Fundamental to all these matters is the distinctive kind of power that ministers wield, power that makes their ethical obligations particularly vital and at the same time can make them harder to fulfill. I lay out the peculiar characteristics of pastoral service that make up professional ethics as it is generally understood—a set of role-specific obligations readily codified as rules to follow—too rigid and shallow to be helpful in a crisis. However correct the proffered standards may be, they are unable to illuminate the inner life on which adherence to all such rules depends. I draw on an older and more profound account of the classical professions, one that understands them as inherently moral enterprises. More broadly, I provide resources for a deeper understanding of the way that human beings who are also ministers can be drawn into corruption by a failure of self-insight, a failure made more likely by a gradual collapse of the disciplines and practices that constitute the sustaining warp and woof of Christian life.

With these matters in view, I begin by discussing the particular character of power as it is exercised by ministers and the recognition of power as a tool of ministry that is both necessary and dangerous (chapter 1). Then I turn to the moral and theological understandings that undergird the ethics of ministry (chapter 2). I argue that pastoral boundaries are to be understood not primarily as rules of professional conduct, but as external signs of deeply rooted disciplines that maintain the emotional and spiritual health required for safe ministry. Nevertheless, such an understanding does give rise to rules, both requirements and prohibitions, and these function as vital bright lines to show when the practice of ministry is compromised and put at risk. Accordingly, I next explore the function of boundaries in ministry and offer practical guidance for maintaining them in the day-to-day work of the pastoral (chapter 3). In the final two chapters—perhaps the most distinctive of the book—I explore the underlying dynamics that make the vital work of spiritual caregiving powerful but also dangerous, and describe the strategies that are most effective at reducing the risk. In chapter 4, I focus on how and why pastors get in the kind of moral and spiritual trouble that can lead to pastoral misconduct, offering warning signs to help them recognize when they are at risk and guidance for how to respond. Finally, in chapter 5, I make a case for the essential spiritual practices that—while providing no guarantee—constitute the strongest barrier against the inner losses that often lead to corruption and failure in ministry.

1

A Moral Framework for Power

We live in a time when the language of power is used often in popular discussion but with quite contradictory inflections. Power is both sought after and feared, praised and decried. Depending on the context, what is meant by the word "power" and how it is viewed by the speaker vary dramatically. Working (as I do) in Washington, DC, one quickly becomes aware of the resonances of the description "politically powerful," which suggests self-interested elites able to manipulate a system toward their own ends. Power seen from this angle is something to be guarded against, something to be monitored and limited to the best of our ability in order to prevent inequity and injustice. We frequently hear of maintaining the balance of power between nations and of the checks and balances put in place by the US Constitution to prevent power from being concentrated in a single branch of government or in the hands of a small group of people. These measures reflect our appraisal of human beings as perennially tempted by power, ever inclined to misuse or overextend legitimate authority to the detriment of others. Some of our most hotly contested public debates have to do with measures to reassign, reallocate, or restrain power in arenas ranging from health care policy to voter registration to campaign finance law. Managing power in the public realm is a constant preoccupation and a constant struggle.

But much attention is also paid to enhancing power, both for individuals and on behalf of groups that are deemed to be disadvantaged or vulnerable. A wealth of self-help literature is aimed at people in various situations and walks of life, coaching them on how to achieve, maintain, and use power in work or social relationships.[1] And a wide array of political movements have the explicit goal of gaining power for people whose economic status, ethnicity, or other characteristics are thought to make them more likely to be harmed or exploited—though there is little consensus regarding which groups really are most vulnerable.

Many definitions of power operate in these conversations, and quite different kinds of power are in view. Therapeutic strategies for those who have been traumatized or abused may focus on recovering the personal power to defend oneself from threats in the environment, whether arising from other persons or from things that may trigger responses of fear or aggression.[2] Feminist activists and writers stress the acceptance and use of personal and institutional power by women, who are often socialized to regard direct exercises of power as domineering and inappropriate. In a different arena, several resources lift up power as a tool of spiritual growth. These may be grounded in a variety of religious faiths and practices or in the teachings of a leader of no particular tradition. They may invoke the power of the Holy Spirit or of meditation or of positive thinking; they may put forward wisdom more or less esoteric about harnessing the power of the spiritual forces of nature or of the ancestors.[3] All of these are offered as paths to greater well-being and peace for human beings, who often experience themselves as beset and beleaguered, pushed one way and another by forces beyond their control. In short, people pursue power in a variety of ways, even while they are often uneasy about it.

1. See, e.g., Angela Duckworth, *Grit: The Power of Passion and Perseverance* (New York: Scribner, 2016); Susan Cain, *Quiet: The Power of Introverts in a World That Can't Stop Talking* (New York: Broadway Books, 2013); Roy Baumeister and John Tierney, *Willpower* (New York: Penguin, 2011).

2. Lucinda Bassett, *From Panic to Power* (New York: HarperCollins, 2001).

3. Neville Goddard, *The Power of Awareness* (New York: Penguin, 2012); Joanne Brocas, *The Power of Angels: Discover How to Connect, Communicate, and Heal with the Angels* (Pompton Plains, NJ: Career Press, 2014); Joel Osteen, *The Power of I Am* (New York: Hachette, 2015).

Ambivalence about power may be particularly strong among those deeply informed by Christian faith, and this ambivalence may pull them in two directions at once. On one hand, Christians are used to thinking of God as omnipotent, and they are accustomed to forms of address that stress divine power. "The Lord of Hosts" and "the Almighty" are familiar and reassuring names for God in prayer and song, inspiring confidence in the believer that the One on whom they call is able to help and sustain them, no matter what circumstances they face. Christians are also formed by biblical texts and liturgies that call on God the Holy Spirit to descend in power on God's people, enabling them to resist evil and transforming them so that they might be signs of the in-breaking of God's power to heal the world. All of this encourages them to view power positively, in terms of its agency for good in a broken world.

On the other hand, Christians are also heirs to the scathing critiques of earthly power, both political and economic, that run through the great Hebrew prophets. These range from the woes pronounced on "those who are at ease in Zion" who "eat lambs from the flock, and fattened calves from the stall" but "are not grieved over the ruin of Joseph" (Amos 6:1, 4, 6) to predictions of all the impositions that would result from the king Israel was determined to have in order to be "like other nations" (1 Sam. 8:4–18). Over and over, the Hebrew Scriptures denounce the arrogance and overreaching that attend the exercise of human power, warning that the abuses of the powerful will bring down judgment on the nations, including Israel and Judah. And for Christians the climax of the biblical witness is the revelation of Jesus the Redeemer, who empties himself of his own power for the sake of those he comes to save (Phil. 2:6–8). He appears not as the conquering hero but as the Suffering Servant, the Lamb of God who "did not open his mouth," even to defend himself before corrupt authorities (Isa. 53:7; Matt. 27:12–14). His advent marks the decisive intervention of the God who "has put down the mighty from their thrones, and exalted those of low degree" (Luke 1:52 RSV), and firmly ties the cause of the Holy One of Israel to those who are despised and powerless.

The unease about power is likely to be especially acute among those who have been to seminary. Theological research over the last fifty years has stressed the degree to which the mission of God in the world is identified with rescuing the marginal and challenging the structures that maintain inequity and foster injustice.[4] Jesus explicitly takes up this mantle at his first public utterance, when he applies Isaiah's words to his own ministry: "The Spirit of the Lord is upon me, because he has anointed me to bring good news to the poor. He has sent me to proclaim release to the captives and recovery of sight to the blind, to let the oppressed go free, to proclaim the year of the Lord's favor" (Luke 4:18–19). No wonder those who aim to follow this itinerant preacher, a man of questionable parentage and no visible means of support, are uncertain about the role of power in Christian life and ministry.

But pastors who wish to align themselves with God's mission, who wish to be of help to the world that God loves, cannot simply dismiss all human power as a manifestation of evil. The broadest and most helpful definition of "power" may come to us not from sociology or political science, but from physics: power is simply the ability to have an effect in the world. In itself, then, power is a kind of capacity, a channeling of energy that makes it possible to bring about a change. Only those who are content to be ineffectual in their ministry can eschew power altogether or regard it as inherently tainted. Thus the key questions, the ones necessary to any moral evaluation of power, are these: What kind of power is used? By whom? And to what ends is it directed? Only when we have answers to such questions can we determine whether the abstract good that power represents is good in any actual case, that is, whether it is good news for the inhabitants of the world in which it is exercised. To recover a critical appreciation of power as a necessary force for good, we turn below to an older conception of what makes the use of unequal power legitimate. It is an understanding already well developed in pre-Christian antiquity, and it underlies the three classical professions of ministry, medicine, and law.

Ethics of the Professions

In the contemporary context, anyone who wishes to draw on professional ethics as a source of insight must overcome several hurdles.

---

4. Two seminal works on this topic are Gustavo Gutiérrez, *A Theology of Liberation: History, Politics, and Salvation*, rev. ed. (Maryknoll, NY: Orbis, 1988); and James H. Cone, *God of the Oppressed*, rev. ed. (Maryknoll, NY: Orbis, 1997).

To begin with, today we use the word "professional" to designate anyone who is paid for any sort of activity, from landscape design to pet photography. It is possible to be a professional house-painter or skateboarder, or even a professional escort (bringing to mind the phrase "the world's oldest profession," a euphemism for prostitution). With the bar for what we mean by a profession set so low, it is no surprise that we often take "professional ethics" to mean no more than the application of lowest-common-denominator standards of decent behavior to the arena of paid work. Thus we might expect to find in manuals on professional ethics minimal requirements of honest exchange and prohibitions on force and fraud, perhaps with some aspirations to basic competence thrown in for good measure. And in general we would not be far off. But embedded in the word "professional" is the trace of the term's origin in the verb "to profess"—that is, to declare publicly one's central convictions and commitments. This is a clue to a much older and richer understanding of certain kinds of human work, one that regards them as fundamentally moral enterprises demanding far more than the minimum of decent behavior.

Underlying the classical professions is the ideal of service to fundamental human needs, needs that require the development of specialized knowledge and skills to address. The acquisition of such knowledge and skills is a prolonged and labor-intensive process. It demands focused study over a number of years and a substantial period of supervised practice. These preparations must be supplemented by ongoing education so that practitioners remain well informed about emerging knowledge in their fields. Since it is not possible for everyone to acquire the requisite knowledge and skills—and indeed not possible for anyone to become expert in all three arenas—all human beings must sometimes depend on the services of professionals to meet essential needs, including the need for spiritual health and salvation, for bodily health and life, and for the maintenance of justice among humans and between them and their societies. Dedication to meeting these needs is the moral foundation of the three original professions of ministry, medicine, and law.[5]

---

5. The following discussion is indebted to the account offered in Richard M. Gula, *Ethics in Pastoral Ministry* (New York: Paulist Press, 1996), 51–64.

The disparate knowledge and skills possessed by the professional regarding a basic human need create an imbalance of power between the practitioner and those served in a critical area. It is one thing for a student's tennis instructor to know more about his or her game than the student does, but it is quite another for someone's physician to know more about his or her body and how to treat it than that patient does. The latter is potentially a matter of health and survival. Similarly, the expertise of the minister may have a bearing on the eternal welfare of a congregant's soul, as the knowledge and skills of the attorney may be needed to preserve a client's property, liberty, or even life. The moral justification for the cultivation and application of this disparate power in other people's lives is the protection of the interests of the patient, congregant, or client. This entails that the interests of those served must govern, direct, and limit the use of the professional's power.

But laypeople in any given arena will not be able to assess fully either the competence or the moral performance of the professional to whom they entrust these basic and critical needs. In churches, laypeople do not usually know enough pastoral theology to judge whether the pastoral counselor gives sound spiritual advice, nor are they in a position to know whether the minister is scrupulous and careful in the performance of professional duties. In seeking medical care, patients are generally not able to evaluate independently the medical knowledge and clinical judgment of their doctor, nor to tell whether she or he has done diligent research to identify the best possible treatment plan. Similarly in law, the average client is unable to interpret either the language of legal documents or the significance of legal proceedings. In all these cases, those who turn to professionals for help are in a significant sense at the mercy of those whom they consult. Those seeking help must depend not only on the professionals' knowledge and skills but also on the professionals' diligence, compassion, and dedication to the good they are trained to serve. That is to say, they must depend on the character of these strangers who wield enormous power over them at times when they may be extremely vulnerable. For this reason the practice of the professions has historically been understood as an inherently moral undertaking. It is not merely a means of livelihood but a dedicated way of life. With this understanding come the five requisite characteristics that distinguish a profession from other forms of compensated work.

Competence

The first requirement of the professions is competence, which involves the specialized knowledge and skills that enable the professional to meet basic human needs—knowledge and skills that must be acquired and maintained at the highest level. The need for professional competence makes ongoing study a moral obligation, an expectation codified in continuing education requirements for maintaining professional licensing.

Moral Commitment

The second central requirement of the professions is moral commitment. The professional must embody a commitment to the good to be served, whether salvation, health, or justice. This is a matter of conviction and personal dedication as well as knowledge and skill. It is not enough to have the required abilities; the professional also must be the right kind of person and care about the right things. This commitment is expected to shape one's whole being. A profession is not just a kind of work; it is a kind of life. Thus professional licenses can be forfeited for moral unfitness or misconduct even if it is unrelated to the individual's work.

Self-Monitoring

Since only those possessed of the requisite knowledge can evaluate the competence of professionals and the performance of their work, the third requirement of the professions is self-monitoring. Professions must have standards of preparation and practice internal to their membership and must provide mechanisms for evaluating and holding one another accountable to those standards of knowledge, skill, and behavior. This requirement for self-monitoring is maintained in bodies of professional licensing and adjudication, such as boards of ministry, state medical boards, and state bar associations.

Altruism

The fourth central requirement of the professions is altruism. The commitment to the well-being of congregants, patients, or clients includes placing their interests above the self-interest of the professional. The form of life of a professional is expected to cost the practitioner something, to entail some degree of sacrifice on behalf of the good of those served. Doctors, for example, are not only expected to be available in emergencies at all hours of the day and night; they are also expected to care for patients even when these patients pose a risk of infection to the doctor. The willingness to make such sacrifices when they are called for is a core element of the moral commitment a professional undertakes. Correspondingly, it is the foundation of the high esteem in which devoted professionals are held by society.[6]

Fiduciary Responsibility

We have said that professionals attend to essential human needs, that they possess vital knowledge not shared by others, and that their work involves the exercise of power in relation to people who may be especially vulnerable. We have noted the requirements of altruism and devotion to the well-being of others. Together, these features of their work entail that the power professionals wield must be rigorously directed to the interests of those they serve and not to the professionals' own interests or needs. The obligations that arise from this duty include the scrupulous honoring of confidentiality and the active and intentional protection of the congregant, patient, or client from harm, whether by act or omission. For these reasons, the kind of power exercised by professionals is called "fiduciary power." It is a term rooted in *fides*, the Latin word for "faith," because it represents a power entrusted for the sake of the one served and not that of the one exercising power. Fiduciary power is not power over another person but power *for* him or her, exercised at the beneficiary's behest, and on his or her behalf. Thus the final requirement of the professions is fiduciary responsibility, the commitment to use entrusted power appropriately.

6. In Washington, DC, one feels compelled to note that lawyers, who are ubiquitous here as lobbyists and corporate litigators, are frequently not well regarded. However, one need only look to journalistic coverage of major criminal trials or the media's treatment of attorneys who represent the indigent or the victimized to see the other side: such lawyers are often lionized and regarded as crusaders for justice. Many of them deserve this regard, for much public good depends on their integrity and commitment.

Ministry as a (Peculiar) Profession

Thinking of ministry in light of the traditional requirements of professional ethics offers us several insights. Each of the distinctive marks of the professions has implications for how ministry is prepared for and practiced, and for what excellence in that practice requires. First, the nature of professions as grounded in special knowledge in service to human need creates an obligation for ministers to become and remain well informed and well equipped for their work. This means that theological education cannot be finished in seminary. Ministers must set aside time for reading and study, continuing education events, and consultation with others when particular expertise is needed for some aspect of their pastoral work. This is not a luxury but a duty to those they serve.

The idea that professional practice requires a personal commitment to the good to be served and a certain character on the part of the practitioner underscores that preparation for ministry can never be merely a matter of information and technique, a body of knowledge and skill that anyone might acquire and employ. Preparation for ministry rests equally on moral formation and spiritual development. Pastors must not only know the right things; they must *love* the right things and become the sort of people who can truly be shepherds to souls. Theological schools and their students must take the spiritual-formation aspects of pastoral preparation seriously. And since character is not only expressed in behavior but also continually molded by it, the work of formation must be recognized as ongoing, a path to which one is committed rather than a destination one reaches.

The necessity of professions maintaining internal standards of accountability means that those who judge the suitability of candidates for ministry and those who evaluate their readiness for service must be prepared to say no as well as yes. Likewise, the church boards and officers charged with monitoring professional performance—particularly those members who are themselves ministers—need to regard their work as bearing responsibility for the welfare of the whole church. To take this responsibility seriously demands the willingness to remove those who for whatever reason are incompetent in, or unfit for, ministry. It is not grace to look the other way—not for the community that is badly served nor even for the person who is thereby abetted in doing harm to the people of God. Jesus's unflinching words about the fate of those who "put a stumbling block before one of these little ones who believe" in him come to mind (Matt. 18:6; cf. Mark 9:42; Luke 17:2).

If altruism is the virtue central to all professional practice, for Christian ministers this virtue has a particular character and a personal name. The love of God made known in Jesus Christ is the touchstone of Christian existence. Accordingly, Jesus is the definitive model of self-giving love, something made explicit in the New Testament: "We know love by this," says the writer of 1 John, "that he laid down his life for us—and we ought to lay down our lives for one another" (1 John 3:16). While such an admonition is addressed to the whole church, it has a particular bearing on life in ministry: those who are called as pastors are to imitate the Good Shepherd, who "lays down his life for the sheep" (John 10:12). Few pastors in the contemporary church may be called on for such literal self-sacrifice (although that depends greatly on where and whom they serve). But even in settings of relative safety, the steady work of being present for and attentive to the needs of others, of resisting the corrosive powers of disillusionment, discouragement, and simple fatigue, can be demanding and costly. For those who aim to sustain such a self-giving pattern for a lifetime, more than good rules of practice are needed. Ministers must be deeply formed in a love that imitates the love of God.

The concept of fiduciary responsibility has a particular resonance in the ethics of ministry. As with all professionals, pastors' ability to help others depends on the trust of those they serve. Such trust includes the confidence that those who have greater knowledge will not use it to do harm, or for their own convenience, or carelessly—but will use it to help the vulnerable who must rely on them. But in the case of clergy, congregants' trust in the pastor is often closely aligned with their trust in God, so that their trust has a religious quality. Though it may not be wise to identify ministers too closely with the God whom they serve, the fact remains that many people see their pastor as God's representative. This is especially the case with people in trouble, who sometimes entrust themselves to a minister's care without reservation. In view of Christian convictions about the pervasive and insidious quality of sin, all who wield such power should be wary of the inclinations to self-serving and self-deception that all humans share. To be invested with authority as a servant of God calls for the most careful self-scrutiny and for scrupulous attention to how, and to what ends, power is used.

Thus far I have focused on the ways in which ministry is like the other classical professions, so that its practice can be illuminated by the ethical requirements common to them all. This is true even though the work of religious professionals contains special elements that give the application of those requirements a particular inflection, as the above discussion indicates. But there are also important dissimilarities between pastoral practice and the work of other professionals, including differences in the particular character of the power that operates and its associations. These bring with them a distinctive set of challenges and risks.

The first of these dissimilarities has already been alluded to. Only in ministry is there the dimension of sacral authority, a power viewed by the community as grounded in transcendent claims and ultimate commitments. For the religiously serious, the stakes can be extremely high. Therefore, ministers are never simply individuals. They are understood to represent a religious tradition and to speak out of an authority much older and broader than their personal insights or opinions. In many cases, they are taken more or less to speak for the whole church or even for God. Many people grant their judgments and advice a (sometimes unreasonably) high degree of deference, which helps to explain how those who intentionally abuse religious authority are sometimes able to get away with it for so long without being called to account.[7]

Allied with the formal, institutionally conferred power of the pastoral office and the authority based on their knowledge of the tradition they represent, ministers are invested with symbolic power. They are visible signs of faith and piety, presumed to be especially close to God, and taken as models of faithful discipleship. Often ministers have ascribed to them virtues and traits they do not actually possess—or at least do not possess in the measure attributed. They are taken to

---

7. See, e.g., Diana R. Garland and Christen Argueta, "How Clergy Sexual Misconduct Happens: A Qualitative Study of First-Hand Accounts," *Social Work and Christianity* 37 (2010): 1–27.

be wise and holy people because that is what their work suggests. It is common for young children to confuse the pastor whom they see with God whom they do not, imagining (for instance) that God must be tall and have red hair because that is what Father Flynn looks like. Such simple associations might cause adults to smile, but even adults who surely know better sometimes harbor a similar confusion. The judgment of the minister is taken without reservation to indicate divine judgment, and the minister's approval or disapproval is equated with the approval or disapproval of God. Such associations are most likely to occur among those who are most vulnerable, people under duress or in pain who feel the greatest need for a tangible support system. This overidentification between the pastor and God is an element frequently found in the most egregious cases of pastoral abuse.

Finally, ministers often bear what might be called projected power, the psychological identification of the pastor with whatever figure of authority and trust a particular parishioner is inclined to turn to for guidance: a parent, a teacher or mentor, or even another pastor from an earlier and more dependent period in the congregant's life. Such projections are particularly easy to apply to ministers for those who encounter them chiefly in their most public roles, as leaders in worship. In public worship settings, the individuality of the pastor may be obscured to some extent by the robes of the office and the structured elements of the liturgy. Depending on the character of the projected relationship for which the minister is a "screen," projection can greatly increase the power the minister wields over the parishioner and can bring an inappropriate set of expectations to bear on the pastor's role.

All these forms of pastoral power are informal, not officially assigned by any institution. They are also not automatic and uniform, but depend on a number of variables in both pastor and parishioner.[8] Rather than being strictly rational and intentional in their operation, such forms of power may be at work subliminally, not fully recognized or even conscious. This makes them harder to analyze and thus harder to govern. Together they constitute an added layer of responsibility

8. For instance, other forms of personal power, such as eloquence, attractiveness, charm, and the ability to empathize, are allied with and contribute to the symbolic and projected power ministers may wield. Likewise, the particular history and psychology of a congregant plays a role in how the minister is seen and received.

and risk in the exercise of the minister's office. Ministers need to be aware of, and careful about, the effect of such dynamics in their relationships with those they serve.

Navigating Unmarked Territory

In addition to the distinctive dimensions of power that attend it, ministry is distinguished from other realms of professional service by its relative lack of contextual role markers. The clearest way to show what this means is by contrasting ministry with other professions. Consider the ordinary setting of medical practice for comparison. When you visit your physician, you go to an office, where you wait alongside other patients who are there for the same purpose. Your doctor is at work, usually with other physicians, in a suite of examining rooms, attended by nursing and support staff. She or he is usually wearing a white coat over business clothing and will likely have a stethoscope around the neck and a handful of tongue depressors stuck in a pocket. You are wearing street clothes or perhaps a cloth or paper examination gown. You meet in a consultation or examination room with quite particular furnishings and equipment that could be mistaken for no other kind of office. Your interaction with your doctor is focused entirely on matters relevant to your health, whether a particular complaint or your general well-being. When the examination and conversation are finished, you shake hands and depart, perhaps with a prescription, some orders for laboratory work, or some counsel about diet and exercise.

Everything about the encounter reinforces the nature, purpose, and limits of the relationship between physician and patient. This is not to suggest that such interactions must be chilly or perfunctory; the doctor's manner and conversation may be warm and concerned, full of human care and compassion. But no one would mistake a visit to the doctor for a meeting between friends to catch up on family news. And ordinarily this professional connection is the only kind of association you have with your physician. As part of their training in ethics, doctors are strongly cautioned against treating friends or family members because it is thought to compromise their clinical judgment and objectivity.

A similar description could be given of what you experience when you consult an attorney or a psychotherapist: there are signals everywhere of the character of the relationship and of what is expected of both parties within it. These professionals are also warned against entering into what are called "dual relationships," situations where they attempt to serve professionally someone with whom they also maintain a personal connection as a friend or relative or even someone whose services they rely on in another context. Such dual relationships are thought to interfere with the quality of the professional service offered and to risk dangerous conflicts of interest. All this is taken with such seriousness that efforts to develop another kind of connection with a responsible professional—say, by asking questions about his or her personal life—are likely to be politely but firmly deflected. (A therapist I know responds to even the most basic inquiries about herself with, "Let's talk about why you want to know.")

Such well-marked professional terrain contrasts sharply with the character and dimensions of relationships between ministers and those whom they serve, particularly in congregational settings. Even the most casual Sunday-morning-only attender will see the pastor at a minimum as worship leader, preacher, and official greeter at the close of the service—a set of roles that call for rather different aspects of social presentation. Moreover, it is a rare preacher who reveals nothing about herself in the course of a sermon, whether that is through illustrative anecdotes, in references to life events, or simply by the way a text is interpreted or a topic chosen. Preaching is by its nature always a triangulation between text, situation, and speaker; it is not the Word of God simply but the Word of God in *this* passage, for *this* time and community, as brought by *this* messenger. Therefore, whether directly or indirectly, preaching always discloses the messenger to some degree, often in deeply revealing ways inasmuch as the preacher speaks of what is near the center of her or his own life's commitments.

If a congregant makes the modest investment of stopping by coffee hour after the service, a whole new world of personal information opens up. If the pastor has a family, at least some family members are likely to be present and known to most of the congregation. Within minutes, any one of a dozen people (like those serving the coffee) can share the names of any of the pastor's children, where they go to school, and which ones are the most rambunctious. Conversation in the fellowship hall often covers recent news in the church or parish, including how long the minister has served there and various tidbits like where the family spends vacations and whether the pastor will play on the church softball team in the summer.

Suppose a member of the congregation becomes involved in the life and mission of the church to any degree. Now there is not only a wealth of additional information about the minister, but also various opportunities for new kinds of interaction and relationship with her or him. There are church projects like cleanup days and church events like bazaars and spaghetti dinners to plan and attend. There are Vacation Bible Schools to prepare for and mission trips involving travel, shared work, and (often) tight sleeping quarters. There are administrative tasks and offices in which members collaborate extensively with the pastoral staff in church leadership. In all these ways, the minister inevitably comes to be known by parishioners in several dimensions: not only in official functions as the pastor but also as a spouse, parent, co-laborer, and so forth. There are still some markers of the minister's official role: clerical collars or robes and stoles for those denominations who use them, for instance. There are also the physical spaces of pulpit and chancel and pastor's study, and the distinctive words and gestures used by ministers leading worship or presiding over sacraments. These are powerful signs of the set-apart character of ministry and are important for that reason. But they are present in only a small portion of the interactions the average minister has with his or her parishioners, especially with those who are most engaged in the church's life.

While other professionals are instructed to avoid any trace of dual relationships with those they serve—and can generally do so[9]— pastors routinely have three or four different kinds of connections with a single congregant. They might cooperate in worship planning on one committee and disagree strongly over a church personnel issue on another, all while playing together on the church softball team. A parishioner might chair the committee that does the annual evaluation of the pastor's performance at the same time that she sees

---

9. Very small towns can be an exception to this generalization, as there may be only a handful of medical and legal professionals who can hardly avoid personal acquaintance with some of their patients or clients.

the pastor for premarital counseling and serves alongside him on the Habitat for Humanity project. And all these structured interactions are supplemented by less formal activities like flipping burgers together at the church picnic or participating in a fierce water balloon fight at the youth group all-nighter. Ministry takes place amid a messy, complicated, many-stranded set of overlapping relationships. It is not a field in which the standard professional model—a single, neatly and narrowly bounded kind of contact between a professional who controls the interaction and a client who receives professional services (and a bill!)—can be readily applied.

One might suppose that this means the warnings that other professionals receive about relationships in which personal and professional roles are commingled do not pertain to ministry. But in reality such warnings are even more important in ministry than in the other professions. Because of the complex and multidimensional character of pastoral relationships, confusion about the minister's role is much more likely, both for the congregants and for the pastor. In the absence of external structures to define and reinforce the nature of the interaction, the inward awareness of obligations and limits maintained by the pastor becomes vitally important. It keeps the real nature of the relationship always in view, reminding the pastor of the disparity in power that exists between ministers and their congregants, and of the unequal responsibility ministers bear to protect those congregants' interests. The distinctions between professional and personal relationships prevent either party from distorting the relation between ministers and congregants with expectations that should properly be met elsewhere. Taken together, these distinctions and the practical safeguards that protect them preserve the space within which ministry can safely happen and parishioners' spiritual needs can safely be met.

At the same time, such barriers are more difficult to establish and maintain in ministry than in the other professions. Not only are the lines between personal and professional relationships not "built in" to the context of pastoral service, as it were, but many aspects of that context encourage confusion between the two. Ministers not only work on behalf of their parishioners; they work alongside them. They not only exercise the authority of their knowledge and expertise from a position of confidence and security like doctors and lawyers;

they also live highly visible lives in a community where they must acknowledge human weakness and fallibility as part of their central proclamation. (The good news that we all have a Savior depends for its intelligibility on the realization that we all—ministers included—need saving.) They are personally known by the communities they serve and must be personally present and invested in order to do their work. Finally, pastors are engaged in leadership not only while busy in serious work but also in the shared laughter and play that mark the life of any healthy congregation, which can make them at times seem like just one among a group of peers. Yet they are never simply members of those communities, nor are they ever simply themselves as individuals. They are always pastors, representing a faith tradition and charged with the spiritual care and guidance of the congregation. Congregants may be inclined to forget this, but ministers must not.

Dangerous Power

There is another reason those who practice ministry need to maintain a clear-eyed and constant awareness of the nature of their role. The work of a pastor requires the exercise of dangerous forms of power: the power that comes of being privy to intensely personal information and the power of emotional intimacy created by pastoral service. I treat these related themes in turn.

Information

Access to private information and the general duty of confidentiality that goes with it are responsibilities all professionals share. However, these responsibilities have added significance in ministry. Whereas a doctor must guard information pertaining to patients' bodily health, and an attorney must keep secret whatever was learned in the process of attending to a client's legal needs, a minister must guard a wide range of information about the lives of parishioners. In the ordinary course of their work, pastors learn who is planning to marry—and frequently who is contemplating divorce. They often know which parents are gravely worried about one of their children, or conversely which adult children are struggling with how to care for their elderly parents. They are consulted by people in all kinds of trouble, from financial difficulties to crises of faith, from substance abuse to crippling grief. The pastor's office is frequently the place where signs of severe family problems like violence or addiction first become evident. And ministers often serve as confessors, listening to the sins (both real and imagined) that burden people's souls, and to the losses and regrets that haunt their lives. The care of a congregation takes one into deep waters.

Since our most painful issues generally involve not only our own lives but also those of others close to us, it is significant that ministers are often acquainted with the families and friends of those whose secrets they carry. They will know many of their parishioners' connections simply by being located within the social community of the church. Casual or inadvertent disclosure of information in this setting is potentially very destructive. It is much more likely to be destructive than, for example, the elevator chitchat among staff that bedevils hospitals. But the point is not merely that disclosure may be harmful: a minister should not divulge confidential information even when convinced it will bring about the best result. Except in very extraordinary situations—where a child, an incompetent adult, or an unwitting victim cannot otherwise be protected from grave harm—divulging such information constitutes a misuse of the pastor's authority and can do irreparable damage to the trust that ministry requires.[10]

At times observing such constraints can be difficult. It is not altogether uncommon, for instance, for a parishioner to confess to the minister an extramarital affair with another member of the congregation, and for the pastor to know and regularly encounter all four of the married adults as well as their children. Even in such challenging circumstances, the content of the confession must be strictly protected. This remains true no matter how vigorously the pastor may admonish the congregant to break off the relationship and even possibly to admit the affair him- or herself.[11] Even if disclosure really is the best course,

10. For a more complete treatment of the circumstances that might warrant or require breaching confidentiality, see Sondra Wheeler, *The Minister as Moral Theologian: Ethical Dimensions of Pastoral Leadership* (Grand Rapids: Baker Academic, 2017), 100–102.

11. While a full discussion of this issue is beyond the scope of this chapter, here I simply note that the question of whether to disclose infidelity to a spouse is complicated and debatable, admitting of no simple and uniform answers. There are

the information entrusted is still rightfully under the congregant's control, and a responsible pastor must not unilaterally decide to share it without consent. Not only are professional obligations at stake; so too is the ability to serve the whole community. A minister cannot meet the spiritual needs of his or her congregants (including the need to be recalled from an irresponsible and destructive path!) without being a safe guardian of information that is given in confidence. Any breach of trust will cut off the vital spiritual ministries of confession and moral counsel that are essential to good pastoral care, not only for the congregant in question but for all who learn of it.

Intimacy

Alongside the power that comes from information shared by congregants, a special power of emotional intimacy comes with the territory of ministry. Ministers are present at key times in people's lives. They are there to welcome new children into the community in infant baptism or dedication, and there to mark the maturing of those same children when they are old enough to make a profession of faith at confirmation or believer's baptism. They witness and bless the union of lives in ceremonies of Christian marriage, and they celebrate the lives and mark the passing of those who have died. In all these ways, pastors share in and honor the times of major transitions in people's lives, whether these are joyous or sorrowful or (as is often the case) both at once. They stand alongside the family and friends who gather for such momentous events, and by word and presence they help to interpret the changes of life within a community united by faith. On such ritual occasions, pastors are there to celebrate or to comfort, to embody and speak time-honored words that connect what is happening in one life to the lives of those who have gone before and those who will follow. Ministers are thus woven into the fabric of meaning and memory that make up a human story, and in that way are drawn into intimate connection.

Pastors are present in times of crisis as well—times of shock or loss, times when the doctor's news is grim or the wandering child is lost beyond recall. They come when the things and people congregants

---

powerful arguments in both directions, and the best course may depend on a number of variables particular to each case.

have counted on fail, when a job they thought was their identity is suddenly gone or the friend and partner they trusted without question turns out to have betrayed that trust and deceived them. Likewise, pastors show up when congregants themselves have disappointed and betrayed others and are confronted with unwelcome new knowledge about who and what they are. And if they are good pastors, they come when others withdraw—when even close friends avoid being near because they have no idea what to say. In times of darkness or doubt, of crushing grief or rage, or of bitter self-reproach, a pastor consoles and accompanies—sometimes with word or touch but often simply by remaining present, a mute testimony to the truth that God does not abandon his people, whatever they do or suffer.

Any pastor of long service can tell what a difficult but also what a holy thing this is: to be present in the depths of human experience, when despair looms and it is not possible to see any future beyond the darkness of loss. Sharing such moments is a privilege and a trust, and those who do share them are ushered into a kind of intimacy known only by the closest and most trusted friends. People share a bond with those ministers who walk with them through the deepest and most painful challenges of their lives, a bond that endures even years after the path is traveled and the crisis is past. With that bond comes enormous power—and corresponding responsibility.

The powers of information and intimacy cannot be separated from ministry, for a pastor cannot do her or his most basic job without becoming privy to confidences, nor fulfill the responsibilities of the office without daring to stand beside people in critical moments of their lives. These powers are simply indispensable aspects of the pastorate. Yet, like symbolic and projected power, they are not formally conferred by an institution and so cannot be revoked by the same. They operate as part of the complex and delicate web of relationships between people that are the stuff of the church and its ministry. They are of enormous value, but they also carry great potential for harm if they are misused. Moreover, these distinctive forms of pastoral power can be abused not only intentionally, out of callousness or malice, but also unintentionally: by oversight or carelessness or because the pastor lacks the self-awareness to recognize when there has been a shift from using these powers to meet the needs of parishioners to using them to meet the pastor's own needs. There is no simple technique for eliminating the risk of such misuse, no set of rules or regulations that can guarantee these relational powers will not be distorted or misdirected. But there are helpful ideas and strategies—ways of understanding and practicing ministry that make its necessary powers less dangerous. These begin with paying attention to the asymmetrical character of relationships between pastors and congregants.

The Challenges of Asymmetry

The most basic characteristic of human relationships is that they are reciprocal. One person extends a hand in greeting, and the other person grasps it. In conversation, each person both listens and speaks. In the polite social advances that mark the beginning of an acquaintance, one person says something about herself and invites the other person to do the same. Often a minimal acknowledgment, the barest smile or nod, is exchanged even by strangers on the street. Reciprocity seems to be an impulse built into us: a healthy infant only a few months old will smile in response to a smiling face. Even non-acknowledgment— the avoidance of direct eye contact on a crowded subway car, for instance—often represents a sort of unspoken social agreement, serving to reduce the discomfort of such close physical proximity among strangers. The process of learning how to enter into workable, positive connections with other people is called socialization, a central task of growing up. People who lack the ability or willingness to negotiate such exchanges, or who are unable to read the cues of a particular society about how they are expected to behave, seem odd to us, awkward at best and rude or hostile at worst.

What applies in casual or fleeting social contacts is more pronounced and significant in intimate relationships that are central to our lives as human beings. In friendship, we both give and receive the blessings of affection and support. In romantic relationships, we are delighted by and seek to delight our partners in turn. Where such reciprocity is not found to some degree, we would not speak of a friendship or a romantic partnership at all (although we might speak of a love that was not returned—a source of sadness rather than of joy). Close relationships are mutual, and their gifts flow in both directions.

At the same time, not all close relationships are between equals who can reasonably expect the same things from one another. Few bonds rival the intimacy and intensity of the connection between parents and their young children, for example, but the relationship between parent and child is one of profound inequality in a number of dimensions. Both parents and children might be said to owe one another certain things—care and protection on one side, for instance, and respect and gratitude on the other—but what is owed is quite different, reflecting the differences in power and responsibility that define the relationship. While we would find it strange and troubling if parents were not protective of their young children, we would also find it troubling if young children felt they needed to protect their parents. When such distortions or reversals occur, we take them as signs that something has gone badly wrong, either internal to the relationship or in the external circumstances that surround it.

The distinctive challenges of relationships between ministers and congregants arise from the fact that divergent characteristics of human interaction are combined in them. On one hand, there are aspects of equality with adult members of the community, the ordinary reciprocity of social exchanges with other adults. Depending on a pastor's length of service and a parishioner's degree of involvement in the church, pastor and parishioner may interact often and know each other quite well, so that such reciprocal exchanges are commonplace. On the other hand, the relationship is not *fully* reciprocal: the pastor who helps with the transitions and crises of congregants' lives does not properly expect the same service from them. There remain basic disparities of power and role that define the relation between minister and congregant. Put simply, the pastor is there to serve the parishioner, but the reverse is not true. In the use of authority and influence, in the sharing of information and experience, in the way in which the connection between the two is developed and maintained, the needs and interests of the congregant and not those of the pastor must govern. It is the minister's professional responsibility to see that this remains the case, and thus a fundamental asymmetry lies at the heart of the relationship.

This does not mean that there will be *no* aspects of mutuality between ministers and congregants. A pastor and congregant may well like one another, share interests, and enjoy each other's company. A parishioner may make gestures of kindness and support when a pastor is facing some special challenge: a thoughtful note on the occasion of a parent's death or a casserole when a new baby disrupts the family's regular meal preparation. But unlike ordinary friendships—where mutual enjoyment and mutual aid define the relationship and care naturally flows in both directions more or less equally—the relationship between pastor and congregant involves important distinctions and limits that must be observed. These limits exist to preserve a space within which ministry is safeguarded. A minister must be careful not to shift the foundation of a relationship with a parishioner from pastoral service to personal liking. This is both for the sake of that parishioner, and for the sake of others with whom such a ready personal connection does not exist. It is vital that congregants be clear about the nature of the connection and the basis on which the pastor is offering care or counsel: as a servant of God and a representative of the wider community of faith.

The disparity of power and the distinction of roles between pastor and congregant help explain why friendship as traditionally understood is a problematic model for that relationship. Odd as it may seem, this remains true even in cases where personal affection and enjoyment are naturally present. To explain this, I draw on the work of Aristotle, whose treatment of friendship as an aspect of moral life remains formative in the West.[12] Aristotle distinguishes between three kinds of connections: with those who benefit us, with those who share some important characteristic or task with us, and with those who are simply part of the same political community. He calls these kinds of associations friendships of a sort: friendships of utility, friendships of interest, and civic friendships. But all of these are relatively superficial ties, and they can be expected to change or dissolve with changing circumstances.

In his writing on character formation, Aristotle focuses on a fourth kind of friendship: friendships of virtue. These are the bonds between people who are bound by mutual trust and brought together by admiration for one another's best qualities. These ties are much more enduring than other kinds of human connection or friendship. Most

---

12. Aristotle, *Nicomachean Ethics*, trans. Terence Irwin, 2nd ed. (Indianapolis: Hackett, 1999), 119–52.

deeply, such friends share a common vision of what a good person and a good life are about, and they help one another to attain that vision. For this reason, these relationships shape who and what the friends become. Those who are friends on this level share each other's lives, both the joys and the burdens. They help one another in need, and their relationship is characterized by complete honesty and full mutual disclosure. The friend, Aristotle says in summary, "is another self."[13] For all these reasons, Aristotle argues, friendships of virtue can only be formed between equals, where disparities of power and role do not interfere with or distort the relationship.

In our cultural context, we often use the word "friend" quite loosely. We may mean by it anything from our closest and most intimate companions in life, to the neighbor we chat with casually at the grocery store, to the 672 people to whom we have given access to our Facebook postings. Certainly in its more general senses, where we mean to indicate only acquaintance, positive feeling, and some measure of enjoyment, there is no concern about friendliness between pastors and congregants. I am not suggesting that pastors should maintain a formal and aloof attitude toward the people they care for, or avoid any kind of social interaction with them. (Such an approach, although not uncommon in the other professions, is neither practical nor desirable in ministry.) But establishing more profound friendships—the kind that Aristotle describes (and that many lonely pastors long for)—with a member of the congregation is likely to create several problems.

First, such a friendship confuses the nature of the pastor's connection with that congregant/friend, making it more difficult to provide spiritual care and guidance based on the faith they share and his or her office as pastor. If a situation arises in which this congregant sorely needs admonition, the clear and challenging counsel of one who speaks from the wisdom of the church, where will she or he turn? If the pastor tries to render such service despite the special friendship formed with the congregant, from whom will the congregant be hearing? The minister of Jesus Christ? Or the congregant's good friend Bill? Ironically, by forming deep friendships with congregants, ministers may unwittingly deprive those friends of a pastor in a time of crisis.

13. Ibid., 149.

Second, having special bonds within the community creates a division. When the pastor creates an inner circle of a few congregants who are also friends, this inevitably creates an outer ring of those who are not so chosen and invited. Often hurt feelings and resentments arise to fracture the congregation and poison ministry.

Third, the obligations of confidentiality that belong to the office of pastor are likely to be compromised by close friendships within the congregation. Nothing is more natural than to tell a friend the things one is thinking about and struggling with. For a pastor who is devoted and serious about ministry, these thoughts and struggles cannot avoid including aspects of the ministry. But a parishioner cannot properly be a pastor's confidant, especially regarding issues or conflicts within the community. Even if the pastor *does* manage to guard the confidences and protect the privacy of other congregants, these congregants may not be sure of that, and their willingness to come to the pastor for help will thereby be diminished because of their uncertainty.

In all these ways and more, ministers who form close friendships with members of the community put at risk their ability to serve well the people God has entrusted to their care. This is a risk they should not take.

Attending to the asymmetry of power and responsibility between ministers and those they serve, and to the moral constraints that arise because of it, recalls the distinctive obligations of those who exercise fiduciary power. Given the vulnerability of people who seek professional services and the potentially destructive power held by those who care for their needs for health, justice, and salvation, those whose work is based on trust in such vital matters are bound to high standards of conduct. Though adherence to these standards may protect professionals and the institutions in which they are embedded, this is not their primary function. Rather, they are designed first and foremost to protect patients, clients, and congregants. This primary concern for the good of others, the preference for their interests over those of the professional, is the very hallmark of professional service and the heart of the ethical duties of professionals. Nowhere is this more significant than in ministry, where breaches of trust can do lasting harm to a person's very soul, damaging that person's ability to love and trust God.

Ethical standards for the practice of ministry can be expressed in a variety of ways: in formal codes of ethics, in official denominational rules, through training in professional ethics required of ministers in a particular tradition, and so on. The lines and limits proposed may have varying degrees of detail and specificity. Insofar as these forms of instruction provide clear standards and rationales for the ethical conduct of clergy, they are beneficial. But in order to help those professionals who are at risk and to prevent harm to those they serve, we must have more than rules. We also need more than policies for responding to violations—policies that are inevitably shaped by litigation and aimed partly at institutional self-protection and minimizing liability. For professional boundaries to protect the holy work of ministry, they must function as the outward markers of more profound moral understandings and be undergirded by disciplines that sustain the emotional, spiritual, and moral health of pastors. In chapter 2, we turn to these deeper foundations for sustaining ministry.

2

Laying Deeper Ethical Foundations

Much of the current conversation about the ethics of ministry is framed in terms of things ministers should not do. In keeping with the metaphor of boundaries, ethical obligations are thought of as a series of lines not to be crossed and presented as a set of rules (sometimes more gently called "guidelines") designed to keep clergy from getting into moral trouble. These rules also aim to protect the institutions within which ministry takes place—churches, schools, hospitals, counseling centers, and so forth—from charges of negligence or the toleration of exploitation and abuse. In view of the revelations of the last few decades—including massive financial frauds perpetrated by so-called ministries and scandals involving serial sexual abuse and high-level ecclesiastical cover-ups across a range of denominations—the desire for clear rules is understandable.

Rule-based approaches also offer real benefits. Clarity about the minimal ethical obligations of ministry, explicit statements of policies and prohibitions, and carefully drafted formal procedures for dealing with violations or allegations of misconduct are important for a number of reasons. They express a clear consensus about what conduct is out of bounds, making it harder for ministers to deceive themselves and others about the most egregious wrongdoing. They help to create a climate in which transgressions are more likely to be reported and dealt with. They also provide a structure for legal accountability, both for perpetrators and for the institutions that have sometimes overlooked or shielded their actions. Explicit "best practice" guidelines and policies may also help ministers whose behavior is entirely innocent to avoid the appearance of misconduct. This may protect them and their churches from the destructiveness of misunderstandings and also from false allegations, which are rare but not unheard of.

For all these reasons, many denominational leaders and several scholars in the field of pastoral ethics favor the creation of formal codes of ethics for ministry, analogous to the codes that govern medicine and law.[1] Some of these advocates have drafted proposals, and a number of denominations have adopted at least some of these written standards as part of their training or certification of clergy.[2] Along with rules prohibiting romantic or sexual relationships between pastors and congregants, codes of professional ethics for ministers commonly address the requirements and limits of pastoral confidentiality and legal and ethical standards for handling church finances and property—partly because these are arenas where grave failures have occurred in the recent past, and partly because they deal with matters in which obligations can be set out in clearly defined rules.

A few sources also provide broader practical guidance, including recommendations regarding settings for pastoral counseling and policies for hiring and supervising staff. Some offer standards for the treatment of personal gifts and provide expectations for how relationships with former parishioners are to be managed when a pastor has moved to a new church.[3] In these matters of broader

1. For comparison, see the Hippocratic Oath, the Code of Ethics of the American Medical Association, the Code of Conduct of the American Psychological Association, and the Ethical Code of the American Bar Association, all available online by searching the given title. For Christian ethicists who recommend or offer ethical codes for ministers, see, e.g., William H. Willimon, *Calling and Character: Virtues of the Ordained Life* (Nashville: Abingdon, 2000); Richard M. Gula, *Ethics in Pastoral Ministry* (New York: Paulist Press, 1996); Joseph E. Bush, *Gentle Shepherding: Pastoral Ethics and Leadership* (St. Louis: Chalice, 2008); Joe E. Trull and James E. Carter, *Ministerial Ethics: Moral Formation for Church Leaders*, 2nd ed. (Grand Rapids: Baker Academic, 2004).

2. Trull and Carter include several examples in appendices; see *Ministerial Ethics*, 217–63.

3. For instance, the Ordained Minister's Code of the United Church of Christ and the Clergy Manual for Practice of the United Methodist Church.

ethical guidance for ministers, clarity and formality are beneficial as they highlight areas of potential sensitivity or risk and provide a common basis for moral reflection and judgment. In all these ways, clear norms of conduct are helpful for training pastors. Accordingly, in the next chapter, I consider ethical standards for the practice of ministry, weigh in on debates about particular issues, and discuss the vital protective function that explicit rules and clear prohibitions can serve in moral life.

But I am not persuaded that codes of ministerial ethics can accomplish everything for which their advocates hope. This is because I do not believe that pastoral misconduct typically occurs because pastors do not understand what their ethical obligations are or why they apply. We can leave aside predators and deliberate frauds who prey on the church—these are wolves masquerading as shepherds, who are hardly likely to be swayed by clearer statements of their moral duties in any case. But research suggests that most ministers who are guilty of ethical violations wander or fall into wrongdoing rather than setting out to perpetrate it.[4]

Vulnerability to misconduct, I believe, arises less frequently from insufficient information or bad intentions than from inner losses: senses of emptiness or insignificance in ministers' own lives that leave them looking for ways to feel appreciated, effective, and powerful. Therefore it does not seem to me that codes of conduct can get at the underlying issues that cause moral failure among ministers. In the face of the profound and universal human hunger to feel valued and prized, to see ourselves as worthwhile and important, I fear that lists of obligations will prove too weak. Especially when we are under pressure or in crisis, rules do not maintain their hold on us unless we see clearly how they work to defend the things we cherish. Detached from the goods they serve, from the things we love and strive for, prohibitions seem arbitrary and irrelevant, and we persuade ourselves that they are not binding on us when push comes to shove. In particular, rules alone will not stand against that most basic of all human losses, loss of the ability to find meaning in our own experience.

4. Marie M. Fortune, *Is Nothing Sacred? When Sex Invades the Pastoral Relationship* (San Francisco: HarperSanFrancisco, 1989), 47, 156n1; Stanley J. Grenz and Roy D. Bell, *Betrayal of Trust: Confronting and Preventing Clergy Sexual Misconduct*, 2nd ed. (Grand Rapids: Baker Books, 2001), 4–44.

My judgment that codes of ethics are likely to prove inadequate has two implications for ministry. First, the moral obligations of ministers must be framed positively before they are put forward as prohibitions. It is the things we embrace and pursue in our lives that animate us, that give us purpose and joy and determination, not those things we forgo in order to obtain what we prize. The moral boundaries that surround and protect ministry must be understood first and foremost as aids rather than constraints. They are the structures within which it is possible to respond faithfully to God's call to serve a community, and thus to become what we are meant to be. To shed light on the affirmative approach I am recommending, in the next section I take what may seem a surprising detour into a discussion of how we talk about ethics. This is because the language we habitually use shapes how we see moral existence, and thus what we are likely to see or to overlook.

The second implication is that the limits we *do* establish, the things we agree not to practice or seek within the sphere of our professional service, must be matched by positive commitments if we are to hold fast to them. These commitments include all the healthy disciplines that nurture body, mind, and spirit—ways of living that nourish us and keep us whole. Only with such practices in place can we be clear-headed and clear-sighted enough to say no to what must be refused in order that we may hear and echo God's unfailing *Yes!* to all that is truly good. Later in this chapter I take up the matter of sustaining personal practices.

Reclaiming a Richer Language

In the modern Western world, two forms of ethical language predominate, profoundly shaping how we understand moral life.[5] The one that tends to occur to us first when the subject of ethics arises is the language of commandments or rules—statements that express things we are supposed to do or not do. In this category belong particular commands, whether positive or negative: "Honor your

5. For a more detailed discussion of these languages and of the theories of ethics they depend on, see Sondra Wheeler, *The Minister as Moral Theologian: Ethical Dimensions of Pastoral Leadership* (Grand Rapids: Baker Academic, 2017), 12–25.

father and your mother" (Exod. 20:12), "You shall not steal" (Exod. 12:15), and so on. Also in this category are more general imperatives: "Love one another with mutual affection" (Rom. 12:10), "Do not be conformed to this world" (Rom. 12:2), and so on.[6] This category is also where we place systematic statements of obligation, like codes of ethics or bodies of legislation. Formally this approach to ethics is called deontological, from the Greek word for duty.

The second kind of language—formally called consequentialism—is used more often when people are asked to resolve a conflict or to choose a course of action where there are various goods to be sought or bad outcomes to be avoided. Here contemporary Westerners are likely to speak in terms of weighing the pros and cons of various possible choices and trying to find the decision that produces the most good or causes the least amount of harm.

These ways of thinking and speaking shape both our public and our private lives. We order not only our national societies but also the smaller organizations and associations we live in by means of laws. Every corporation, nonprofit organization, and even local garden club has by-laws that specify what is permitted or forbidden, required or optional. Central personal relationships like marriage and parenthood are also partly shaped by law, as well as by promises that aim to specify what duties each party owes the other. Once a promise in such an arena is made, it creates a new rule of action: we owe fidelity to a spouse, care into adulthood for an adopted child, loyalty to a friend, and so on. The language of obligation is everywhere.

At the same time, social policy and practices large and small are frequently decided based on calculations of what will deliver the best outcome. Tax codes, traffic controls, zoning laws and development planning, public education initiatives, vaccination requirements—all are devised using complex projections about what will get the best result using limited resources and causing the least interference with individual preferences. Such calculations come into play in private life as well. When faced with a murky or difficult personal decision, many of us weigh pros and cons, laying out the good and bad consequences we expect to follow from one course of action or another.

6. Here I have chosen biblical examples, but it would be just as easy to provide imperatives from secular philosophy or law.

To the extent that the good and bad results we weigh have to do with our well-being and that of those affected by our actions, what we are doing is a kind of consequentialist moral analysis.

These ways of thinking about moral life have much to offer, and people ordinarily use both of these strategies when making decisions. We consider which obligations are binding on us as well as which practical outcomes are at stake, for good and ill, in our choices. Despite the differences between them, these two moral languages have one thing in common: they focus on the particular decision a person or community confronts at a given time and ask what is the right or best thing to do in that situation. Therefore, the results of this kind of ethical reflection are called "action guides," conclusions about how to behave in the case at hand, and they are indispensable.

However, for our purposes I want to draw attention to a third kind of moral language, called the ethics of virtue or character. This approach, too, has a long history in the West, although it has come into and gone out of fashion repeatedly over the centuries. Virtue ethics pays attention to the long-term course of a person's life, considering how individual acts reflect and contribute to who that person *is* and to who she or he *will become*.

The central difference between virtue ethics and other approaches to moral understanding is that virtue ethics focuses less on an individual decision and more on the decision-maker. Rather than concentrating on a single moment in time, it looks at the overall pattern of acts, judgments, and commitments that make up a person's life story and in which we read her or his character. Particular decisions and actions still matter according to the ethics of virtue; they still have effects in the world as well as in the person acting and can still be judged as morally right or wrong. But individual decisions are understood not chiefly in themselves, as the application of a rule or the result of a calculation of benefits and harms. Instead they are seen as an expression of and a contribution to more basic and enduring aspects of the person who acts.

According to virtue ethics, actions cannot rightly be judged in isolation. They make sense and find their significance as part of a larger story, the story of what a person is trying to be and do. It is only in light of that larger story that we can properly evaluate any single act. Is it courage or foolhardiness that causes a pilot to attempt a risky takeoff in bad weather? Is a blunt answer to a socially awkward question an expression of honesty, or indifference, or just the unthinking candor of childhood? Is a soft reply to an insult the result of holy humility or the meekness of the habitually bullied? The truth is, without knowing more of the story, we cannot tell. This dependence on a broader framework for evaluation applies to one's own choices as well, for the meaning of any decision is known only by its place in a larger narrative: the story of what one is pursuing and who one is becoming in this act.

The insistence upon a narrative context for judgment is grounded in the original definition of a virtue as a trait that equips a person to attain his or her ends, to become what he or she is meant to be. And therein lies the challenge for those who would use this approach in contemporary life. If there is anything about which there is no agreement in the modern world, it is the point or purpose of a human life—what we are here for. Law, literature, philosophy, politics, popular culture, and even advertising all offer competing answers, but we are rightfully suspicious of most of them. The prevailing view seems to be that there *is* no point, nothing that humans are "meant to be" beyond whatever any individual might choose to provide meaning solely for himself or herself. And this helps explain why the ethics of virtue has fallen out of use in public discourse.

In classical moral thought, virtues were understood to serve like the rudders on a boat, which enable it to go where the captain intends. Prudence is the skill that enables the navigator to set the right course. The virtues of justice, courage, and temperance are aids to navigation; they eliminate obstacles and confusions—in the form of biases, fears, and desires—so that the pilot can steer true to the course marked out by prudent judgment. But lacking a destination, navigation is pointless. Without an overarching purpose or any idea of what we are trying to do or become, there is no way to define virtue and nothing by which to guide judgment or evaluate character. The only question we can ask of any person's commitments is whether they were freely entered into and are "authentic" in the sense of being his or her own.

We still have the words for virtues and vices and still use them to praise or criticize someone's character. But in a moral landscape where we share no account of what we are here for, there is no way to judge whether a trait is truly a virtue in the original sense of equipping a person to achieve her true end. Therefore, such terms are often used in ways that are biased and without objective content.[7] A person we like with a strong personality is assertive; a person we don't like is a bully. If we share someone's commitment, he is determined; if not, he is stubborn. We call someone we love trusting; we call a stranger gullible. Examples can be multiplied. Is a person gentle or weak? Resolute or heedless? Forgiving or a doormat? Once these words become unmoored from any shared understanding of what a good human life looks like or aims toward, they can do little more than express our feelings toward someone. No wonder public moral discussion tends to be shaped in terms of specifiable obligations and desirable outcomes rather than in the language of character.[8]

If late modernity (including its recent offspring, postmodernity) lacks a goal to give order and conviction to moral life, this need not be true of the church. Indeed, it *cannot* be true—not unless the church has conceded its identity and reason for being to the surrounding culture for redefinition. If the church continues to understand itself as the community of those called by God into a new life in Jesus Christ, if its purpose is to announce the good news of God's reign and to be a sign of that reign breaking into the world, then we have better questions to ask of ourselves and one another than whether our moral choices are "authentic" or not. Instead, we ask whether the decisions we make further the purpose of our lives as ministers of reconciliation (2 Cor. 5:18) and whether the character we cultivate conforms to the image of Christ each of us is called on to become (Rom. 8:29; 2 Cor. 3:18).

To guide these judgments, the church has a wealth of concrete rules of action. Drawing on Ephesians 4 alone, we get "Speak the truth"; "Do not let the sun go down on your anger"; "Thieves must give up stealing"; "Let no evil talk come out of your mouths"; and "Be kind to one another, tenderhearted, forgiving one another" (Eph. 4:25–32). But Christians also have a model to imitate that gives life and unity

7. For a full discussion of this phenomenon, consult Alasdair MacIntyre, *After Virtue: A Study in Moral Theory*, 3rd. ed. (Notre Dame, IN: University of Notre Dame Press, 2007).

8. One exception to this generality is political campaign speech, which makes much use of language about character. Unfortunately, its use there is also an arch example of the lack of fairness and objectivity that makes such language suspect.

to all such rules: "For you know the grace of our Lord Jesus Christ, that though he was rich, yet for your sake he became poor, so that by his poverty you might become rich" (2 Cor. 8:9, RSV). And this model also provides Christians a goal to aim for: like Jesus, we aim for the joy that is set before us (Heb.12:2), to be fitted for eternal communion with God and the saints.

This overarching understanding makes it possible for the church to use all three forms of moral language in ways that avoid being arbitrary or circular. Rules make sense and have their claims on us because they are not just imposed by some authority, but are grounded in who and what we are trying to become. The good consequences we seek to realize in particular choices are good not simply because we choose them, but because they are part of the welfare of a whole community that is called together in mutual love and service. Striving for these ends represents our own small part in the mission of God in the world. The virtues we lift up are recognized as virtues because they equip us for the form of life that is our fulfillment as well as our duty. In all these ways, the intelligibility and coherence of Christian moral life is founded on the story we believe, the story of redemption offered in Jesus Christ. This is how we know what is true and important, what is worth living and striving for: we are here to be restored to fullness of life as the images of God we were created to be and to become signs and instruments of the coming reign of God. Ultimately, as an old catechism puts it, we seek to be renewed in God's likeness so that we may "glorify God and enjoy him forever."[9]

With this discussion of ethical language as background, we can say more clearly what it means to approach pastoral ethics positively. It means seeing the moral boundaries that enable ministry as a form of life to be embraced and inhabited rather than a series of lines not to be transgressed for fear of personal and professional disaster. If morality is understood as being at heart a path toward fulfillment, a way of realizing the deepest truth of one's being, then we are drawn on by possibilities rather than held back by restrictions. Instead of beginning with things that must not be done, we begin with the high privilege of a call to serve the church of Jesus Christ. We receive this call for what it is: an invitation to enter into the very life of God,

---

9. Westminster Shorter Catechism, answer to question 1.

who is present among us as one who serves. It is for the sake of this calling that ministers undertake a life of discipline and integrity. At the same time, those who have taken to heart the gospel's message do so in full awareness of their own limits and brokenness as well as their gifts. Therefore, they acknowledge gladly their human finitude and their continual reliance on all that God provides to nurture, heal, and sustain them. All human beings share this need for sustenance, but those who would be servants of God must especially recognize and honor it. This recognition has a host of implications for moral life in ministry, which I explore in the remainder of this chapter.

Honoring the Needs That Make Us Human

Relationality

We start from the understanding that ministry is the furthest thing in the world from a solo undertaking. From the outset, those who enter on this path draw on the wisdom of those who have gone before them—the words of prophets, apostles, and saints (living and dead), who testify to the truth and share the fruit of their own walk with God. Candidates in training work with others to prepare themselves by study and reflection as well as by practice and imitation of the best models they can find. They continue throughout the duration of their ministry to read and reflect and to confer and collaborate with colleagues, working to develop and refine the skills they need to preach, teach, and offer help and counsel. And throughout all their years of service, they strive to live before the people they serve lives that are "worthy of the calling to which [they] have been called" (Eph. 4:1), knowing that all the sound instruction in the world will lead only to cynicism if it is contradicted by example. But if they have truly been formed by the tradition in which they have been schooled, then they also know this: such a life is not a possibility that lies within their power if they only try hard enough or study the right books. The clarity of vision and singleness of heart that keeps ministers on the path is the work of the Holy Spirit. This Spirit is made present to us in Word and worship, and in all the individual practices of Christian faith—but also through the presence, nurture, advice, and support of others.

For ministers, these others include the teachers who help them recognize and prepare for the work they are called to do and the mentors and supervisors who guide and watch over that work. They also include their colleagues in ministry, both those in immediate partnership and those encountered through larger regional or denominational associations. All these people have the advantage of sharing the specialized knowledge that undergirds pastoral work and the benefit of their own experience as a source of insight. They can give counsel and offer empathy and encouragement when pastors become frustrated or demoralized, a state that anyone who remains long in ministry can expect to struggle with at times. A person who hopes to sustain this challenging form of life in a way that is healthy and fruitful over time must seek out and cultivate strong relationships with clergy colleagues. Even the apostles who had walked with Jesus were sent out to minister in pairs.

But the needs of ministers are not limited to those for professional support and assistance. The women and men who are ordained or commissioned to lead the church, called to act as shepherds to their sisters and brothers, remain still women and men. Like all human beings, they came into the world helpless, dependent on the care and protection of other people for mere survival. Like all humans, they continued for many years to rely on others for nurture, instruction, and socialization, until they reached the degree of maturity that allowed them to make their own decisions and pursue their own interests in relative independence. But even now that they have reached adulthood, they continue like all human beings to need other people in myriad ways, ways so deeply ingrained in all of us that we hardly pay attention to them. We begin here, with basic needs we take for granted and rarely reflect upon.

In the midst of God's pronouncements on the goodness of creation in Genesis, one statement stands out: "It is not good that the human creature should be alone" (Gen. 2:18, altered). Even in paradise, in a communion with God yet unclouded by sin, it is not good for the human to be without human companionship—the most fundamental of all human social needs. So profound and universal is this need that even those imprisoned for terrible crimes against their fellows, who might be thought beyond all positive connection to other people, show signs of severe mental illness when maintained in solitary confinement for long periods.[10] Some minimal degree of contact with other people seems to be required for human beings to maintain a sense of their own reality and identity.

Beyond the bare necessities of psychological survival, we rely on other people for modeling and affirmation, for we are so deeply constituted as social creatures that we only learn how to function normally as human beings in relation to others. From infancy onward, our day-to-day engagement with and responses from the people around us form the ideas and patterns that guide our behavior. We absorb over time the ways of behaving and reacting that enable us to live as members of a human community, and receive the reinforcement that makes that participation rewarding. This process continues our whole lives. Even in the most routine human encounters—brief interactions with store clerks and letter carriers or casual exchanges with neighbors in the supermarket—we continue to be shaped and fed. Human existence is social existence.

In addition to these basic human interactions, the deeper relationships we develop with our peers supply much of our sense of personal identity and significance. The labor we share with others connects us to the human undertakings that give our lives a sense of purpose and direction. Through collaboration, partnership, teamwork, and even competition, our ability to be creative and productive is enhanced, and our ability to withstand the pressures or frustrations of our working lives is sustained. This is true even of seemingly solitary activities, such as research or writing. Good writers admit that their work is a form of conversation in which one draws on and responds to the thoughts and ideas of others across time and space. Nothing is more social than the life of the writer, for thinking and coming to new insights are inherently collective enterprises.

Finally, from relationships with those closest to us—family members and the partners and friends who deeply share our lives—we

10. Jeffrey L. Metzner and Jamie Fellner, "Solitary Confinement and Mental Illness in U.S. Prisons: A Challenge for Medical Ethics," *Journal of the American Academy of Psychiatry and the Law* 38 (2010): 104–8. Juan Mendez, United Nations rapporteur on torture, in a 2011 report to the secretary general, found such isolation to be a form of psychological torture, among the inhuman and degrading conditions forbidden by international protocols on the treatment of prisoners. There is a movement among prison reformers to have solitary confinement declared an inherently "cruel and unusual punishment" and so proscribed by the US Constitution.

draw much of what gives our lives richness and meaning. These primary connections are the source of our most profound satisfactions and our keenest joys. Here we find our sense of being valued and prized, of being lovable and worthwhile because we are loved and we love in return. Accordingly, threats to these relationships cause us the greatest anxiety and pain. Above the barest level of physical survival, these bonds and the people we share them with are the things we live for, and live on, at least on the human level. To lose them is devastating, and it requires something like rebuilding the self to go on after such a loss.

Of course, people sometimes have to live without a network of healthy relationships at all these levels. But we normally think of those who are prevented by outward circumstances or inner limitations from establishing significant connections to other humans as profoundly deprived. And people who are living through the breakdown or loss of a primary relationship suffer in proportion to its centrality in their lives. Everyone can expect to go through periods of acute struggle, times when the relationships they depend on are seriously troubled or conflicted. Likewise, everyone who lives long enough will see at least some of their connections with those closest to them severed by separation or death. These are times of deep loneliness and vulnerability. We can endure such losses, but no one would call the prolonged grief that follows the breakdown of a central relationship or the death of a loved one an experience of well-being. Humans may be able to survive a degree of isolation, but human flourishing is relational.

So far I have treated the profoundly social and interdependent nature of human existence as a simple fact. It is something we find to be true about ourselves from introspection and observation as well as through the formal study of human development and psychology. From the perspective of natural science, human sociality is like any other aspect of human being: a feature that develops by accident and is retained and passed on because it confers some adaptive benefit. The idea that social existence is something pressed on us by our need to survive is reflected in the work of seventeenth-century secular philosopher Thomas Hobbes, who is famous for his dour view of human society. Hobbes regarded human interdependence as an unhappy fact, and human cooperation as a concession to necessity. In Hobbes's view, society is merely the grudging accommodation of the sovereign individual to practical constraints. Life outside of some social order, he acknowledged, "is solitary, poor, nasty, brutish, and short."[11] For this reason, he recommended the acceptance of a social contract whereby we can agree to cooperate to the extent required but with the least possible constraint on individual liberty. For Hobbes, social life is something we put up with for the sake of our lives as individuals.

But to Christians, who understand human beings as creatures of God, the facts of our nature, including the adaptive advantages of interpersonal bonding and cooperation, are not mere accidents. They are reflections not only of God's creative intention but also of God's own trinitarian nature. Humankind is made in God's likeness. As the inner life of God is being-in-relation—the eternal communion of Father, Son, and Holy Spirit—so God has made humans so that they thrive only in relation to one another. To acknowledge that God has made us so that we need one another, not by accident but according to God's good purpose, is to view our dependence on others as not a limit but a gift and a blessing. As the persons of the Trinity have their unity and being in the joy of holy charity, so are we literally made for love. As we are made in the image of a God who *is* love (1 John 4:8, 16), our flourishing as human beings involves intimate connection with others. We therefore give thanks for this aspect of being human, despite the risks, messes, challenges, and heartbreaks that accompany it. And we honor God's intention by remembering and taking account of our need for human companions.

Embodiment

We in the developed West live in the midst of odd contradictions. In many ways we give more attention to the human body than ever before in recorded history. Through the intensive study of molecular biology and genetics, biochemistry and physiology, we know vastly more about the development and functioning of the body than our predecessors. As a result, we are able to intervene in bodily processes more comprehensively and successfully than could have been imagined even a few decades ago. Doctors can prevent, manage, or cure

11. Thomas Hobbes, *Leviathan*, ed. Edwin Curley (Indianapolis: Hackett, 1994), 76 (1.13).

once-devastating illnesses, and these capacities continue to expand rapidly. Beyond the sphere of scientific medicine, there is a wealth of resources on how to maintain physical vitality and optimal health. The marketplace presents a plethora of vitamins and food supplements, diet and exercise plans, and programs of meditation and relaxation aimed at minimizing stress. A casual stroll through the self-help section of any bookstore reveals the variety of options on offer.

In addition, there is an enormous interest and investment in the appearance of the body, something that bears only a slender connection to the pursuit of health. Industries representing tens of billions of dollars in economic activity are devoted to the design and manufacture of fashionable clothing, shoes, and accessories. Other companies produce a continuous stream of new cosmetics and products for decorating fingernails or styling hair, enhancing the complexion or reducing the signs of aging. And apart from the enterprises that provide these products or services, a whole secondary tier of businesses exists to promote and sell them: advertising agencies, marketing consultants, magazines filled with advertisements, television commercials, and even morning "news" programs that are themselves thinly veiled commercials, featuring the hottest celebrity touting the newest product or style.

But for all this attention to our physical selves, other aspects of life and culture in the twenty-first-century West suggest a profound neglect of our bodies and the things they require to remain healthy. Most American adults, for example, get too little sleep and even less relaxation. On average, they spend less time with friends and family—including in activities like playing with their children—than in previous generations. They also get inadequate exercise, even in the modest form of walking. And these patterns continue in spite of widely published research showing the life-shortening effects of sleep deprivation and constant stress, and the health risks of physical inactivity.[12]

12. The CDC reported in 2016 that between 35 percent and 40 percent of Americans meet the clinical definition of sleep-deprived, getting less than the minimum of seven hours of sleep per night. The reported average is 6.8 hours versus the normal daily sleep need of seven to nine hours for adults ("1 in 3 Adults Don't Get Enough Sleep," https://www.cdc.gov/media/releases/2016/p0215-enough-sleep.html). The average American reports spending less than 5 percent of their time in relaxation and play

Despite readily available information and advice about good nutrition, modern Americans tend to eat poorly, consuming too much sugar, fat, and highly processed carbohydrates and not enough fruits and vegetables to provide needed vitamins and fiber. This is often a problem among poorer people, both urban and rural, for reasons that have partly to do with the economics and logistics of retail food distribution. Even those who would like to make healthier choices often lack access to fresh food at prices they can afford. But similarly poor eating patterns hold true for many financially comfortable Americans as well, even though they have the resources to maintain a healthy diet and convenient places to purchase fresh food. In combination with a lack of exercise, these eating habits are responsible for an exponential increase in obesity, type-2 diabetes, hypertension, and cardiovascular disease—conditions that are on the rise even among children.[13]

Finally, employed Americans work longer hours than any generation since the first half of the twentieth century, bringing work home evenings and weekends and even devoting much of what is supposed to be vacation time to responding to emails and text messages from bosses and coworkers. The so-called connected generation is never out of touch with the workplace. Increasingly, this around-the-clock availability is an expectation for ordinary workers as well as senior executives in many lines of employment. The resulting lack of balance between work and respite contributes to high rates of stress-related diseases and psychological symptoms, causing a sharp rise in the use of prescription drugs to treat hypertension, anxiety, and depression.[14]

("Study: Americans Not Getting Enough Relaxation Time," http://www.wral.com /study-americans-not-getting-enough-relaxation-time/14092767/). According to the CDC's National Center for Health Statistics, fewer than 21 percent of Americans get the recommended amount of cardiovascular and strengthening exercise (https://www .cdc.gov/nchs/fastats/exercise.htm).

13. See, e.g., Bruce Clark, "The American Diet: A Sweet Way to Die," *Food Safety News*, February 26, 2010, http://www.foodsafetynews.com/2010/02/the-american-diet -a-sweet-way-to-die/. Regarding childhood obesity and associated health risks, see Paul W. Franks et al., "Childhood Obesity, Other Cardiovascular Risk Factors, and Premature Death," *New England Journal of Medicine* 362 (2010): 485–93.

14. Taking into account only hours spent actually away at the workplace, labor researchers Ellen McGrattan and Richard Rogerson report: "Weekly hours per worker . . . decrease between 1950 and 1970 but have increased steadily since, and this increasing pattern has continued in the 1990s" ("Changes in Hours Worked 1950–2000," *Federal Reserve Board Quarterly Review* 28 [2004]: 16). According to another article,

The patterns of our culture affect all of us to some degree. They present unreasonable expectations and unhealthy models that are absorbed, contradictions and all, by those inside as well as outside the church. When medical breakthroughs are promoted on morning talk shows and in supermarket tabloids, it is not hard for laypeople to see modern medicine as a bottomless bag of tricks, one that ought to be able to provide a remedy for every complaint and a solution for every problem. When told our options for medical treatment are exhausted, we cry out to our doctors, "There must be something you can do!" When we run out of conventional treatment options, we explore alternative healing practices. But even when health problems are the result of long-term habits that we knew were unhealthy, we struggle to find the time or motivation to commit to real changes. Instead we are tempted by shortcuts, miracle cures, and foolproof diets promising to take off twenty pounds in ten days. Most of us know better, but still we are influenced by the messages that surround us, often more than we realize.

Bombarded by images of beautiful twenty-somethings wearing the latest styles, we feel that we must compete and may find ourselves investing more time and money in how we look than makes sense even to us. We have trouble accepting gracefully the changes in appearance brought by time, and we look for ways to slow its march or at least to disguise its visible effects. Those of us in middle age often resent the slower pace and reduced physical endurance of a body twenty or thirty years older. Shaped by a culture that idealizes late adolescence, we are intolerant of the limitations of age in others as well as ourselves and regard the natural curve of physical vitality, which rises into early adulthood and gradually declines thereafter, as an obstacle to be overcome. Preoccupied with the vigor of youth, we are less appreciative of the gifts of maturity: the wisdom and perspective given by experience, the richness of enduring friendships, and the joy of welcoming new generations.

But perhaps more than by any other cultural influence, we are seduced by the lure of constant productivity. Church leaders, along

---

adding work done from home dramatically increases hours and stress. See Nick Hellen, "Taking Work Home Is Deadly," *Sunday Times*, February 19, 2017, http://www.thetimes.co.uk/article/taking-work-home-is-deadly-g9zwcvtg5.

with everyone else, eagerly adopt strategies to get more work done in a day, squeezing in a session of email before breakfast, a business meeting over lunch, and phone calls after dinner—if we even stop for meals at all. We want and expect to be "on" all the time, and there are a thousand devices to help us be just that. The technologies that once promised to speed up work and allow increased time for leisure more often make work ever present, and make us ever available to perform it. Many ministers send and respond to messages at all hours and type away on the laptops we increasingly take with us everywhere— even to bed. Again, we know better than this. We encourage for our congregants and for those we supervise a healthier balance of work, rest, and play than we ourselves maintain. As pastors and teachers, we give better advice than we follow in this realm.

The above observations are commonplace and can be found in countless newspaper and magazine articles as well as books and blog posts.[15] It is not hard to see that the way our society understands the human body and the ways it encourages us to treat it are bad for our health and should be resisted on that ground. But for Christians, there are also theological reasons to be critical of modern attitudes toward the body, with their strange mixture of obsession and disdain. Like the view of other human beings as limitations on our freedom, and of relationships as encumbrances to be tolerated for the sake of practical advantages, our culture's view of the body is *untruthful* and therefore causes us to be *unfaithful* to our true calling.

To regard human bodies only as objects of control and management— subject to whatever interventions we can devise to hold illness, aging, and death at bay forever—is to reject bodily life, limitations and all, as the gift of God. To regard them chiefly as tools of self-presentation and self-marketing—so that we are locked in a permanent contest with all others for attractiveness and attention—is to treat even our own bodies as a kind of commodity, and to turn neighbors into competitors. Instead of being the means by which we fully engage with one another and with all of material creation, the body is reduced to a facade, a tool by which we serve our own desires. And to constantly press the body's limits, reaching always for ways to cram more in and

---

15. See, e.g., Mental Health America, "Rest, Relaxation and Exercise," http://www.mentalhealthamerica.net/conditions/rest-relaxation-and-exercise.

get more done, is to denigrate God's wisdom in making us to need cycles of work and sleep and renewal. It is also to flagrantly ignore the command that we honor God's Sabbath rest. In contrast, the Christian tradition teaches that, like our human need for companionship, the human needs and vulnerabilities that come with embodied life are to be received with gratitude and humility.

The Dangers of Denying Basic Needs

Ministers are people, despite the tendency—often shared with those they serve—to forget that obvious fact. It is true that ministers are people who have answered a call from God, and they are rightly held to high standards of personal and professional conduct. Only those who are prepared to serve wholeheartedly, to make real sacrifices, and to steadily place the interests of others before their own have any place pursuing this calling. Still they remain ordinary human beings, sinners in need of grace, and people in need of all the forms of nourishment and care that humans require for health and well-being. They depend on God daily for mercy, for light by which to see the path, and for the strength to follow it. They are nurtured and supported by relationships with other people—friends and family, colleagues and neighbors—and grieve when these relationships are lost. They live in bodies that require food, exercise, and rest, bodies that age, decline, and suffer losses. In short, ministers share the same limitations and vulnerabilities as all others, but these limitations and vulnerabilities have particular implications for the practice of ministry. So we must ask what difference it makes for pastoral ethics to consider the inherently social and embodied character of human existence.

Since it has pleased God to make human beings so that they depend on God, on each other, and on the physical world for sustenance, I argued above that people who deny or minimize any of these facts about themselves make a theological error. But for those who aim to serve God through pastoral ministry, such denials also pose real risks, not only to themselves but also to the people in their care. In chapter 5 I focus at greater length on what it means practically for a pastor to acknowledge and honor his or her constant need for the grace of God. Here I want to focus on the more mundane matters that we have been considering—our need for relationships and our recognition of bodily limitations—since they are perhaps less often stressed when training and preparing candidates for ministry.

To the extent that these matters are discussed in theological education, they are usually handled under the heading of self-care, perhaps in the context of a course on pastoral care and counseling, or on the practice of ministry. Often the language used is of the need to love oneself. This language is perfectly appropriate so far as it goes. There is such a thing as a morally required self-love, which is part of psychological health and also an aspect of honoring God's handiwork, even in oneself. But this language can make ministers' attention to their own social and emotional well-being—and even to their physical health—sound like something they do entirely for their own sakes. It appears only as a form of legitimate self-interest, something to be weighed against the needs and interests of others, especially their congregants.

When the matter is framed in this way—as caring for oneself versus caring for others—it is easy to perceive it as a zero-sum game. Seeing it in this way, the more devoted and serious a minister is about serving God's people, the more likely she or he is to minimize or neglect real personal needs in the urgent desire to do more for those served, whether within a congregation or in a wider community where needs often seem endless. Sometimes this genuine desire becomes confused or complicated by a minister's need to feel important, powerful, or needed—able to come to the rescue. But in fact this kind of distortion is more likely to develop when work crowds out the chance to feel significant and prized in other realms of life, such as relationships with family and friends to whom we are precious and irreplaceable as unique individuals. And even when the passion to be of help remains altogether whole and sincere, understanding self-care as a contest between one's own well-being and the interests of congregants creates a dangerous situation.

There is an obvious danger to the pastor, physically and emotionally exhausted and spiritually undernourished, who is liable to illness, burnout, or collapse. But there is also a danger to the people that pastor serves. For over the long term, in a reasonably healthy human being, basic needs that are neglected for too long will reassert themselves. A body deprived of nutritious food will eventually feed itself on what is unhealthy. The need for rest can only be deferred for so long before the exhausted body falls asleep sitting up or even standing, in the middle of a task or behind the wheel of a car. And the same is true of our human needs for appreciation and affirmation, for friendship, love, and intimacy. If people do not have—or do not permit themselves time to enjoy—legitimate places to meet their needs for affection, approval, and support, they are highly likely in time to seek to meet those needs in other ways. Ministers who ignore their personal needs over an extended period are at greatly increased risk of shifting the patterns of their work—gradually, subtly, and perhaps without even realizing it until it is very late—from doing their best to meet the spiritual needs of their congregants to getting their own needs met through the community they are supposed to serve.

The shift to meeting personal needs through the patterns of one's ministry need not—and initially is not likely to—take the form of overt misconduct or clearly unethical behavior. Rather, it can begin with something as simple as leaving the work of preparing sermons until Saturday night because one is just too worn out to start. Then it becomes a race to prepare for Sunday morning, often resulting in badly prepared or hastily rehashed messages, or even the use of someone else's material pulled off the internet.[16]

Another form of adapting your ministry to meet your own needs is shaping the content of preaching—what texts or topics are chosen and what is said about them—to whatever is likely to bring the most enthusiastic approval from listeners. Of course, attention to the people one is trying to reach is a basic part of effective rhetoric in any setting. A preacher who is altogether indifferent to the ideas and inclinations of a congregation, or not willing to invest the time and care required to win their trust before tackling sensitive issues, is unlikely to have much success in preaching for them. But at some point there must be room for exploring with a community the challenges Scripture places before all of us. There must be a place to bring a difficult message or

16. The latter is not unethical in itself, so long as the use is acknowledged from the start and does not become a regular way of shirking one's own responsibilities. But I have been shocked at reports of how common plagiarism and dishonesty in preaching have become. For more on this, see Robert Stephen Reid and Lucy Lind Hogan, *The Six Deadly Sins of Preaching: Becoming Responsible for the Faith We Proclaim* (Nashville: Abingdon, 2012), 18–22.

to wrestle with a controversial topic.[17] A pastor whose preaching is guided chiefly by what adds to her or his own popularity is no longer performing the office faithfully.

While preaching is the most visible aspect of pastoral ministry, distortions of ministry can appear in other arenas as well. Ministers in congregations and other settings are often administrators of organizations, responsible for recruiting, training, and leading lay volunteers in teaching and service. In larger churches, they also supervise staff, who may be other clergy or educators, musicians, or support staff. They ordinarily work with lay leaders, councils, or boards of deacons or elders in exercising leadership, collaborating in decision making about the life and mission of the church or ministry. And in congregational settings, they normally share the planning of worship and the design of liturgy with other contributors, such as lay readers, choir directors, or organists. In all these roles, ministers are called on to be leaders. They exercise oversight, offer guidance, and share the fruit of their training and experience.

But the job of ministers is not simply to *do* the work of the church, as if they had been hired to "do religion" for the community the way a gardener is hired to do the groundskeeping for a property owner. Neither is the job to make all decisions, treating everyone else as if they were there merely to execute the minister's plans. The real work of pastors is to "equip the saints for the work of ministry" (Eph. 4:12); it is to teach, prepare, and form the members of a community in readiness for the work to which *they* are called and joyfully to welcome them as partners in the gospel of Jesus Christ (cf. Phil. 1:5). In ministry as in parenting, one of the benchmarks of success is that, over time, the minister becomes less and less necessary, as disciples mature and become able to take their own part in the work of the church without the pastor's help.

To realize this goal, the minister must be willing, indeed happy, to step aside. She or he must encourage and strengthen others' work, delegate significant tasks to associates and lay leaders, and help them to recognize and develop new skills and capacities. More than anything else, the minister must be willing to step out of the spotlight

---

17. For a discussion of why and how a preacher might tackle sensitive or challenging topics from the pulpit, see my companion volume, *Minister as Moral Theologian*, 26–58.

and yield the center of attention to others. A minister who believes the pastor must be in on everything, on stage at every event, making every decision, and the one to whom all needs must be referred, has adopted a misshapen view of the church, one that is theologically problematic and at odds with Scripture. To the extent that this pattern is held to in order to feed his or her need to be important, it is already a form of corruption and the abuse of power.[18]

And there are still other ways to distort ministry. Just as entrusted powers can be misused by overreaching, they can also be misused by neglect, carelessness, or misdirection. The less rewarding duties of ministry may be left undone because the emotional needs of the pastor—for appreciation, authority, admiration, and so on—are better served by other activities. Which activities those are depends on the particular personality of the minister. Some will prefer to focus on counseling and visitation, others on chairing important committees, others on preaching or teaching. The important question is this: Whose interests govern the allocation of the minister's working time, and what needs shape the priorities of his or her ministry? Are they the pastor's own, or those of the community?

Along a similar line, the powers that do properly belong to the office of pastor can be used improperly. For instance, a minister seeking to seem "in the know" may share confidential information with others under the guise of pastoral concern, causing trust within the community to suffer. Or a minister may use privileged access to other people's lives to fill the minister's own needs for intimacy and significance instead of the parishioners' needs for counsel and support. This can create in congregants an unhealthy dependency as well as presenting other, potentially graver risks.

It is notable that, with these initial misuses of pastoral power, no obvious lines have been crossed, nor have any of the offenses that commonly make for public scandals been committed. But since the moral justification for the unequal power exercised by ministers is based on the interests of those who are served, which is always to direct its use, something vital has already been lost. Pastoral identity

18. For a wonderfully vivid portrayal of this kind of distortion of ministry in service of ego, see the film *The Apostle*, written and directed by Robert Duvall (1997; London: October Films, 1998), DVD. Duvall also plays the lead.

is being corroded by unmet personal needs of which the minister may not even be fully aware. By such small deflections, the minister gradually turns from serving the community to which she or he is appointed, to being served by it, and this is the beginning of corruption. Moreover, once this initial turn has been made, it becomes more likely that further steps will be taken in the same direction: finding justification for misusing church funds, for instance, or for using information given in trust for the minister's own benefit. Once personal needs are being met through the pastoral office or by relationships with those in the pastor's care, the line between subtle deformations of ministry and more egregious misconduct becomes fainter and easier to cross.

Toward Unselfish Self-Care

I have already said that those who understand themselves as creatures of God, who know their lives to be gifts entrusted to them for God's glory, have a compelling theological reason to take proper care of themselves. "Do you not know that . . . you are not your own? You were bought with a price; therefore glorify God in your body" (1 Cor. 6:19–20). According to Paul, our relation to our own lives is not that of owners but rather that of stewards, those who care for what belongs to another. We are designed to nourish and cherish this bodily life (Eph. 5:29), as we are likewise instructed to nourish and cherish the brothers and sisters we have been given. This is how we learn the shape of love and how we are prepared for the love of God that is our destiny and fulfillment. The writer of 1 John goes so far as to make our love for other people the sure test of our love for God: "Those who do not love a brother or sister whom they have seen, cannot love God whom they have not seen" (4:20). The requirements of caring for our bodies and our relationships are not first and foremost duties owed to ourselves or even to one another; before anything else, they are duties owed to God.

Ministers have yet another set of reasons for taking their created human needs seriously and acting to meet them responsibly. They are looked to as patterns of discipleship, as models for others, examples of what faithfulness looks like in a given time and place. Given the deeply unhealthy attitudes and habits that are part of our cultural context, one aspect of modeling Christian discipleship in the present age is offering a countercultural example. Ministers are in a position to acknowledge and honor the fact that human finitude and mutual dependence are not a concession torn from us by necessity, but a blessing from God. They do this partly by what they teach and preach, but they do it even more compellingly by the life they lead before their people and the patterns they build into the church's common life. They can take time for rest and play, nourish their friendships, and protect time with their families. They can organize church life so that meetings take place in regular and specific windows of time instead of spreading into every day of the week and devouring every available minute. They can lift up and celebrate the gift of Sabbath, teaching by example that the universe can do without our labor for a time, and practicing this sign of our obedient trust in God's abundance as an important safeguard of human well-being and dignity.

Finally, wise ministers take care of their own human needs for the sake of their calling and its integrity, knowing that it is not safe to neglect them. Such practical prudence is already familiar to us. Home economists warn those trying to stay on a budget not to go to the grocery store hungry. Recovering alcoholics are instructed to avoid hanging out in bars. People beginning a weight-loss program are advised not to move in above a bakery. In the same way, people who are steadily depriving themselves of rest, who are starving for a sense of being appreciated and loved, who are seeking to prove to themselves that they are significant and effective, should be cautioned against undertaking a life of service aimed at caring for others' spiritual needs. It is simply too dangerous, too likely to go awry and cause harm to themselves and to others. Therefore, those who believe they are being called by God to ministry must recognize at the same time a calling to all the disciplines of a healthy life: adequate sleep and rest, regular respite and play, nourishing food and moderate exercise, and the cultivation and enjoyment of close and nurturing relationships of affection and intimacy.[19]

Ministers, like all human beings, are made to live an embodied life and made for relationship. Therefore, along with food and sleep, laughter and play, they need the deep rest of being with those who

19. See also my discussion of the equally essential spiritual disciplines in chapter 5.

know them, faults and all, and love them all the same. Ministers too need people who enter into their concerns and struggles just because they are theirs, people for whom they are first of all a particular person and not a representative or a symbol. It is vital for pastors to spend time with those who know them outside the context of ministry, those to whom they are not Reverend or Pastor or Doctor So-and-so, commissioned to serve as leader and example, but simply Susan or Jack: a friend, a partner, a little brother, a member of the bowling league, or the kid voted least likely to succeed back in high school. These relationships where ministers are *not* "the pastor" are essential if ministers are to safeguard all the relationships in which they *are*, where they must be ever aware of the office they hold and the special responsibilities it brings.[20]

In this chapter I have argued that preserving space to meet personal needs in all these ways is vital to ministers' ability to meet their pastoral responsibilities. In chapter 3, we turn to the function of boundaries in preserving the distinction between self-care and pastoral service so that both the long-term welfare of the minister and the integrity of ministry are protected.

20. Not long ago, I was teaching seminary students in Russia, talking with them about the challenges of the "fishbowl" aspects of life in ministry, of feeling always under observation and scrutiny. When the metaphor of a life in a fishbowl proved hard to translate, I drew on the blackboard a picture of a round bowl with a small fish swimming inside, visible from every side. After a break, I returned to the classroom to find that some wise and witty student had erased my fish and replaced it with one who was leaping up out of the bowl, with a broad smile on its face. I was happy to know they had gotten the message.

3

Protecting Space for Ministry

In the previous chapters, I have framed the ethics of ministry in relation to the use of unequal power. In chapter 1, I drew on the ancient understanding of the professions as moral enterprises, ways of life that require unselfishly using knowledge and authority entrusted for the service of essential human needs, and treated the ministry as a particular case of professional service. Accordingly, I discussed how the traditions of professional ethics shed light on the practice of ministry, but also the distinctive challenges that arise because of the complex character of pastoral relationships.

In chapter 2, I placed codes of pastoral ethics in the context of two broader sets of ideas: the ethics of virtue as the positive pursuit of ultimate human fulfillment, and the implications of our having been created as fundamentally interdependent and embodied beings. I argued that only by taking this wider view can we fully understand the depth and subtlety of the ethical challenges that arise in the practice of ministry, and only in this way can we prepare to meet them reliably over many years of service. Contending that the starting point of ethics in ministry must be affirmative, I described the positive disciplines of a healthy life as the practices that equip vulnerable human beings to faithfully shepherd others.

While I have argued that faithful ministry is grounded in a life of virtue and in healthy practices, this does not eliminate a necessary place for the ethics of duty: a set of obligations that proceed from the minister's calling and enable it to be fulfilled. In this chapter, then, we turn to moral norms and standards for the practice of ministry, matters often discussed in contemporary literature in terms of pastoral boundaries.

The Function of Boundaries

The term "boundaries" denotes the limits we put in place to mark off a protected space for ministry. Boundaries exist in order to create an environment where congregants can freely bring their needs and vulnerabilities without fear of being wounded or exploited. In recent years, largely prompted by public scandals and gross improprieties that have come to light over the last three decades, a great deal has been written about how to maintain proper boundaries in ministry. This ranges from advice for safely conducting pastoral visitation in the home to standards for background checks on parish staff working with children. The best of this material includes careful rationales for the ethical duties and prohibitions that come with ministry, and accounts of the devastation that can be wrought in a community by violations of them.[1] Much of this work focuses on avoiding sexual misconduct by ministers, outlining best practices for preventing such abuses and for responding to them when they occur. In this and the following chapters, I build on this work to offer strategies and practical guidance for understanding and reducing risks. But because the term "boundaries" is often used without great clarity, I want to begin with a very basic definition of how I use the term.

In the most general sense, boundaries are lines that mark divisions between things, separating things that cannot be commingled without altering their identity. To take an example from biology, cell walls or membranes constitute the boundaries of a single cell. Complex organisms also have internal structures that separate organs from one another, as well as outer barriers of cellulose or shell, hide or skin that separate the organism as a whole from what is outside it.

1. For a sampling of this literature, see the further reading list.

These boundaries are not altogether impermeable; living things are systems in which each part interacts with the others, and they can only subsist through continual exchanges with their environment. Still, the boundaries of an organism are necessary for its life, and too violent a breach of them is fatal. Likewise, in geography, borders are the boundaries that mark the distinction between one political entity and another. Without the establishment and control of borders, political scientists teach us, a state cannot exist.

In human relationships, boundaries are the lines that distinguish psychologically between one person and another; this distinction is necessary for there to be a relationship between them. Human infants at birth do not initially know where their own bodies end and their mothers' bodies begin, or even that they are separate. In that sense, from the infant's side, there is no "relationship" at the start: there is only sensation.[2] The prolonged journey to achieving personal self-awareness involves coming to understand self and other as distinct but related. These dual processes are what developmental psychologists call "differentiation" (becoming distinct from others) and "attachment" (becoming emotionally connected to others).[3] They are as essential to becoming a functioning human being as the physical development that enables us to act in the material world.

Beyond the basic separation between self and other, as humans mature boundaries also separate what properly belongs within a particular kind of relationship from what does not. All cultures include ideas about what exchanges have their place in a given relationship and how much of the self is to be offered and received in those exchanges. Part of the long-term work of socialization in any culture is learning how human connections are understood there. We learn who counts as a close relation, who is more distant, and who is inside or outside the family, the community, or even the society as a whole.

2. I am drawing here from Margaret Mahler's work on separation-individuation theory. For a basic exposition, see Child Development Media, "Margaret Mahler and Separation-Individuation Theory," http://www.childdevelopmentmedia.com/articles/margaret-mahler-and-separation-individuation-theory/.

3. For a fairly accessible account, see Paul Renn, "Attachment, Security, Separation and Psychological Differentiation," April 15, 2010, http://www.counselling-directory.org.uk/counsellor-articles/attachment-security-separation-and-psychological-differentiation/.

The norms of a society also define how relationships are shaped by factors such as the age, gender, and social role of the participants: what is appropriate, for example, between adults and children, employers and employees, or women and men. Patterns and expectations about relationships are part of the moral and social system that functions within a given human community. While standards of behavior change over time, they tend to do so gradually. These standards help determine the kind and degree of interaction people have with each other, how much personal information they share, and what they expect of one another. Boundaries, then, are the distinctions and separations that help to keep human relationships operating within the moral framework of a society. Boundaries act not only to limit relationships but also to sustain them and to keep them healthy by making clear what is to be looked for in them, and what is owed there.

At the same time, woven throughout the organizing ties of kinship or circumstance that unite people and communities in various ways are the particular connections forged between individuals. Such relationships are generally less well-defined (at least unless they are formalized within marriage or some other structure), and expectations within them are often harder to manage. In the developed world, where there is considerable social mobility and freedom of association, personal attachments sometimes form quite apart from other factors that bind people to one another, which can make for improbable friendships and unlikely liaisons. But more often close personal relationships are predicated on other kinds of connections. Most of the time we find our friends and confidants, romantic partners and enduring companions, among the people we encounter at work or in school, through shared interests and pursuits, or through a common membership in a group or organization we find meaningful.

As we spend time with people we enjoy and share with them activities that are important to us, we naturally become attached to them. Our shared experiences form a bond that may grow into affection, deep friendship, romantic attraction, or eventually even into a settled life partnership. As a personal relationship develops between two people, the borders of what is natural and appropriate between them change. We joke with and tease those to whom we are bound by affection in ways we would not a person with whom we have no such bond. We share with close friends things about ourselves that we would never reveal to a mere acquaintance. Gestures of affection that are welcomed between romantic partners would be altogether offensive if offered to a coworker—or even a good friend—without a clear invitation. The boundaries we observe regarding how we are present with others, what information we share, and how we express our connection (especially through touch) define what kind of relationship we share with them and what can be expected from it. Such boundaries are typically so taken for granted that we do not even stop to think about them.

For practicing Christians, the church is often a setting where they get to know and become attached to others. Church life provides countless occasions for shared learning or discovery, as well as emotionally moving worship, mission activities, and opportunities to care for members of the community who are in difficulty—all of which are natural contexts for intense bonding and forming strong personal connections. The presence of strong relationships between members is one of the signs of health in a congregation or other ministry organization. This makes for a richer but also a more complex emotional landscape, and this is the landscape within which ministry takes place.

Keeping Boundaries Clear

Given the complexity of relationships within the church, ministers face particular challenges in maintaining the professional character of their relationships while at the same time remaining open, friendly, and personally present to their congregants. They naturally form bonds with colleagues with whom they work closely, and they come to like and enjoy many of their congregants. In addition, if they are reasonably successful in ministry, these feelings are often reciprocated. Nevertheless, as I discussed in chapter 1, friendship is a problematic model for relationships between pastors and parishioners or staff members because it presumes an equality of power and responsibility that does not truly obtain there. For similar reasons, romantic or sexual relationships in this context are even more problematic, and such relationships are expressly forbidden in most contemporary codes of pastoral ethics.[4] Well-drawn professional boundaries can preserve a space in which it is possible for a minister to focus on the needs of those seeking pastoral help without seeming impersonal or aloof, and without having to pretend to be a tower of strength who has no need of other people.

In this section I offer guidance for keeping messages about the nature and purpose of ministers' connection with congregants clear and consistent so that parishioners can receive the pastoral care and service they need without confusion or harm. While there can be no guarantees, these strategies help to avoid the ambiguities and moral conflicts that arise when the lines between personal and pastoral relationships, or between personal preferences and professional obligations, become blurred. In accord with that practical purpose, I organize this section according to the issues and challenges that commonly arise in the course of ministry. But before turning to particular strategies, it is helpful first to acknowledge the variety of relationships that develop within any ministry setting.

There are many reasons ministers form different kinds and degrees of relationship with different members of the communities they serve. Some of these are structural. In many forms of congregational organization and in other church-related institutions, the minister works closely with certain individuals and small groups simply because of the offices these people hold. These may be lay leaders or congregational presidents, governing boards or senior deacons, ministry councils or staff-parish committees. Especially in times of challenge or transition, the amount and intensity of time spent working with these leaders can be great, and it can create strong bonds.

4. In their article "How Clergy Sexual Misconduct Happens: A Qualitative Study of First-Hand Accounts," *Social Work and Christianity* 37 (2010): 1–27, Diane R. Garland and Christine Argueta identify thirty-six denominations that have framed rules declaring sexual contact with parishioners or counselees abuse. See, e.g., Clergy Ethics Policy and Procedures for the Christian Church (Disciples of Christ) in Illinois and Wisconsin, https://cciwdisciples.org/wp-content/uploads/2013/06/ClergyEthics PolicyandProcedures.pdf; Sexual Misconduct within Ministerial Relationships in the United Methodist Church, http://www.umc.org/what-we-believe/sexual-misconduct-within-ministerial-relationships; Ethical Guidelines for Presbyterian Ministers, http://www.sangabpres.org/ETHICAL%20GUIDELINES%20FOR%20PRESBY TERIAN%20MINISTER.htm. For a useful selection of such codes, consult Joe E. Trull and James E. Carter, *Ministerial Ethics: Moral Formation for Church Leaders*, 2nd ed. (Grand Rapids: Baker Academic, 2004), 217–63.

Other relationships are the result of circumstance. A congregant might live next door to the parsonage and drop by regularly for casual conversations or neighborly exchanges of local news. Or, at the other end of the spectrum, close relationships with congregants might be formed through family crises, like the serious illness of a child or the sudden death of a young spouse. A responsible pastor will be present to console and accompany the family in such circumstances, and helping them through such a dark time will naturally forge a powerful connection.

Relationships can also develop through shared service and common interests. A person who is consistently active in aspects of church life in which the pastor is directly involved will be better known. The handful of members who faithfully go on the mission trips organized by the minister every summer will have a different relationship with him or her than other congregants will. And closer connections may develop with those who have more in common with the pastor than other members, or who share similar interests.

Moreover, it is natural for ministers to have different feelings toward different congregants. It is unreasonable to expect otherwise in a large and diverse ministry setting like a congregation, a school, or a hospital. People have different personalities, habits, preferences, and gifts, and we all naturally connect with some more easily than others. These personal inclinations are not nullified by the biblical commands to love our sisters and brothers, our neighbors, and even our enemies. While these commands are to be taken with full seriousness, love insofar as it can be commanded refers to an attitude, a discipline, and a pattern of action rather than a spontaneous emotion. The duty to love someone cannot be understood as a duty to like that person (although it might entail a duty to look attentively for things that are likable in him or her!). It is rather the duty to serve a person's true interests to the best of one's ability.

While ministers' relationships with congregants may vary in all these ways, ministers nevertheless have the same basic set of responsibilities toward each of them. Those responsibilities are to lead, to guide, to nurture, and to care for the spiritual growth and well-being of each congregant. These responsibilities must remain the center of every pastoral relationship and must be kept clearly in view by the minister at all times and with every member. This has many implications for how relationships with congregants can be lived out. We turn now to practical strategies for navigating these relationships, organized around issues that arise in the course of ministry.

Negotiating Challenges to Professional Boundaries

Socializing

We have already observed that, in contrast to other kinds of professionals, ministers routinely spend informal social time with the people they also serve as pastor. Church members often joke that any excuse will do for a potluck, and in many congregations it appears impossible to hold a meeting that does not involve sharing food of some sort. Beyond these, a parish may have long-standing and cherished traditions of special social occasions: games or sports, rotating small-group dinners or movie nights, annual picnics or barbeques, annual parties or concerts, talent nights or even full-scale musical productions. These events can be of great importance to members of the community.

To some serious-minded pastors, activities like these may seem beside the point, not really part of the church's work or the pastor's calling. But laughter and play are in themselves healing ministries, and they help to strengthen the human connections that sustain a community of faith and service. A minister who makes a practice of avoiding such social occasions will seem chilly and uninterested, and will be unlikely to win the trust that makes it possible to fulfill his or her official responsibilities of preaching, teaching, pastoral care, and administration. Effective ministry relies on connections with people on many levels, and for this reason interpersonal skills and a reasonable amount of social comfort and poise are essential tools for its practice. It is not necessary for the minister to attend every gathering (which could easily take an unreasonable amount of time), nor must the minister be the life of every party. But it is wise for ministers to support by their presence those things that are prized by their congregants, and to visit a wide enough variety of such events to spend informal time with a broad range of individuals and groups within the community.

In addition to activities that are open to the whole congregation, ministers are often invited to social occasions at the homes of congregants: casual dinners, family celebrations, holiday parties, and so on. Here as well it would be odd and awkward to refuse all such invitations, but in this realm certain issues do arise. First, ministers must bear in mind how they are perceived by others, seeming to have special friends or preferred members singled out from among the congregation. Second, they must consider how the congregants issuing the invitations understand the nature of their relationship with the pastor. Finally, ministers must remember at all times the position they occupy, doing or saying nothing on these occasions that confuses or impairs their ability to fulfill their role, which goes with them in all interactions with congregants.

Negotiating the particular challenges of ministry, as well as the ordinary social expectations of reciprocal invitations, calls for delicacy and judgment. It is wise to avoid a pattern of socializing repeatedly with some congregants while never socializing with others at all. To some extent this depends on others' initiatives, but the minister can take steps to keep matters on a more equal footing, including intentionally forging stronger connections where these are lacking. Pastors can propose a pastoral home visit or an informal meeting at a local coffee shop with congregants they wish to know better. They can also institute new patterns for spending time with smaller groups—for instance, making one or two committee meetings a year into potlucks or backyard barbeques. This provides occasions for socializing that are clearly tied to the work of the church rather than to friendships with particular congregants. Or they might create a cycle of invitations—based on shared interests or areas of service so that conversation flows easily and the character of the event remains clear—that over time will include everyone in the congregation. (The practicality of this approach depends on the size and nature of the community.) Finally, ministers can extend general invitations to personal social events, such as an open house or cookout. Such strategies will not flatten out the differences between people or make all relationships with congregants identical. But attention and care can help to prevent the perception—or the reality—of a privileged inner circle of those close to the pastor and a larger group of those on the outside.

Gifts

Another concern in the ethics of ministry is the question of receiving personal gifts or services (outside of one's contracted compensation) from congregants. These fall into two categories: (1) gifts given to a minister by a particular congregant or family and (2) gifts given by the whole congregation to a minister or her or his family. I will treat these in turn.

Personal gifts from individuals raise many of the issues involved in socializing with particular community members and not others discussed above. A gift known to other members incurs the same risks of resentment or feelings of exclusion that arise from special friendships within the community. There is also some danger of confusing the nature and basis of the pastor-parishioner relationship for the congregant who gives the gift. Both of these risks become more serious when there are large differences in economic resources within the congregation or between some congregants and the minister.

There are further considerations related specifically to receiving gifts as well. Where the gift is of significant monetary value, there is real reason for concern. Accepting an expensive present from a congregant skirts the edge of using one's office for personal benefit, and for that reason is ethically questionable on its face. It also can contribute to an unhealthy pattern within a community, a pattern of those who have more resources having (or expecting to have) more leadership and influence. I have been told more than once of affluent congregants giving a large present to a pastor and expecting special treatment in return, such as having decisions about the church's life go their way or even having a pastor look the other way if the giver's behavior might otherwise call for challenge. These may be extreme cases, but they highlight the potential for moral conflict and corrosion that arises when the responsibility of a minister to care for the interests of others is compromised by self-interest, in reality, or even merely in appearance.

Ministers do well to think in advance about how they will handle these situations. To prevent misunderstandings and hurt feelings, it is wise to have a policy in place, preferably one discussed in advance with whatever committee or church officer is charged with pastor-parish relations. If an outright refusal to accept personal gifts seems ungracious, the minister can establish a limit to the value of a gift she or he will accept. The appropriate amount will vary according to context, but it should be modest enough to be in reach for every member of the community. (As a bonus, it's amazing how much creativity a ten-dollar limit can inspire.) In addition, some kinds of gifts should not be accepted because they are too personal in nature—gifts such as jewelry, most items of clothing (a tie or a winter scarf might be an exception), or personal fragrance—regardless of the expense. Such gifts can suggest a kind of intimacy that is confusing and out of place in the relationship between minister and congregant. Lines can be crossed from either side, but the responsibility for clarifying the true nature of the relationship and restoring the boundaries that mark it belongs always with the minister.[5]

An alternative strategy that avoids any appearance of compromise is adopting a church-wide practice for giving gifts within the community at holidays or birthdays and participating enthusiastically in that exchange. There are countless models. A church might have a random drawing in which each adult congregant gets the name of a person to buy a small gift for, or a church could have a grab-bag type of exchange with a modest amount as a price ceiling. Some churches offer mission fairs or fair-trade opportunities so that congregants can shop for small gifts or make donations in someone's honor that also serve the congregation's missional priorities. Others encourage donating money saved by reducing purchases to fund a single church mission project, naming these funds to celebrate pastors or members whose service has been exemplary. All of these offer ways to express appreciation and fondness within the community without muddying the waters of pastoral relationships or excluding those of limited means.

Gifts given to a minister by the congregation or community as a whole avoid some of the issues raised above, and there are certain occasions, such as the retirement of a long-serving pastor, where such

5. An important exception: it is not unheard of for unwanted personal or romantic attention from a parishioner to reach the level of sexual harassment, where the pastor's clear communication and efforts to reestablish appropriate boundaries are consistently ignored. At this point, it is time to involve church authorities or in some extreme cases even law enforcement officials. It is sad to say, but given the special issues faced by women in ministry, this is something they especially must be careful about.

a collective gift is altogether appropriate. However, communal gifts can raise issues of their own.

First, communal gifts are much more likely to be of substantial monetary value. In some settings, there is even a tradition of giving pastors expensive items, such as high-end clothing or luxury vehicles, that most members of the congregation would not own themselves. This creates an ethically problematic situation in several ways. It draws special attention to the pastor not given to others, it creates a distinction in lifestyle between that minister and most of the congregation, and it suggests that the pastor is being served by the community rather than being devoted to its service.

Second, it is not uncommon for a congregation to solicit special funds for pastoral gifts, which can cause members to feel pressed to make a donation to demonstrate their loyalty to or affection for a pastor. This has the effect of shifting the nature of the pastoral relationship, creating a situation in which the congregant feels obliged to take care of the pastor instead of the pastor taking care of the congregant. Practices of this kind can very easily become corrosive, dangerous to the moral character of the minister and the community alike.

However, the matter of communal gifts or services given to the pastor is often complicated by long-standing patterns in some denominational or cultural contexts, and cherished traditions in particular congregations. These may include observances like an annual celebration of a pastor's service held on the anniversary of her or his coming to the parish, or parties to mark a pastor's birthday or wedding anniversary. Some congregations host a yearly pastor appreciation week, marked by parties, celebratory meals, and gifts.

It is important to understand that many of these practices had their historical origins in times and places in which ministers were paid very little, or not at all. Their original purpose was thus to compensate a pastor who had to work a paying job to make ends meet while putting in long hours on a voluntary basis, cutting short the time available to make a living. There are still many settings in the world, including some in the US, where the situation warrants a special effort on the part of the community to make sure that those who make sacrifices to serve the church are not in actual want. But it does not honor the spirit of these historic customs if they are followed in a way that effectively places the pastor above her or his congregation materially, or makes the unselfish service of ministers look like the pursuit of personal gain or status.

The prestige that properly belongs to ministry comes from the minister's dedication to serving God by serving the church. Pastors should be compensated fairly according to the standards and resources of the community, and their service should be recognized chiefly by the trust and gratitude they earn from those they shepherd. As a general guideline, then, pastors should discourage practices that separate them in status or lifestyle from the congregation, or that mark their personal milestones in ways not extended to other members of the community. They should also be attentive to how the practices of the church appear to outside observers, taking care not to bring the gospel into disrepute by seeming to serve their own interests rather than the Lord.

Emotional Support and Care

Like everyone else, ministers face challenges in their personal lives. They have the worries and conflicts that are an inevitable aspect of family life, and they experience the financial strains that most families deal with at least some of the time. They are as likely as anyone else to endure periods of distance and alienation in their marital relationships—perhaps more so given the tendency of life in ministry to make demands on family time and privacy. They, too, may have children who present the special risks and anxieties of parenting adolescents. (In fact, the usual acting out and rebellion of teenagers are often made more acute by the additional scrutiny that comes with being a preacher's kid.) Ministers also have parents who age and die, just as they themselves confront the changes and challenges that accompany aging, illness, and mortality. And on top of all they have in common with others, ministers often carry with them the added burdens and suffering of congregants in trouble, which can weigh heavily on them as well.

It is perfectly normal to seek support from other people when dealing with significant personal stresses, whether these arise from conflicts that make home feel more like a battleground than a haven, or painful losses that cause loneliness and grief. Seeking help in such times is a sign of maturity and health, an aspect of accepting the human need for relationships discussed in chapter 2. This might involve consulting a counselor or therapist, asking for assistance from a mentor, or simply spending time with close friends who can offer the powerful relief of empathy and a listening ear. None of this is of special concern in ministry, but issues arise quickly when the minister turns to the community she or he is serving to provide the support that is needed. The problem is not that the minister shows human weakness or reveals personal vulnerability. (In fact, such revelations might be very helpful messages for a congregation to receive.) Rather, the problem is the potential to distort the pastoral relationship, reshaping it into one where the congregant must try to meet the pastor's needs instead of the pastor meeting the needs of the congregant. For this reason, care and emotional support in times of personal stress *should* be sought, but outside the setting of ministry rather than within it.

As noted above, this does not mean that ministers must always hide or deny the serious problems they face. Many events, such as the loss of a parent, will ordinarily be known to the whole community. Nor does it mean that parishioners' modest gestures of help or support to a pastor in a trying time must be refused. But there is a difference between accepting a casserole, an occasional evening of babysitting, or an encouraging note, and allowing a congregant to take on the role of caretaker to the pastor. The latter creates role confusion on both sides, and changes the nature of the relationship in unhealthy ways that may not be reversible.

There are some circumstances where a personal challenge is so great that a minister is temporarily unable to fulfill pastoral responsibilities. A serious illness, a devastating personal loss, or a family crisis may require a minister to take personal time, a temporary leave of absence, sick leave, or even an extended sabbatical. In such a case, it is important to communicate clearly to the appropriate church or denominational authorities the nature of the situation and whatever is known about its duration. A truthful explanation for an absence should also be given to the members of the congregation, though it is important to carefully consider how much information ought to be shared.

Often a basic and general account is best: *I find I need to take some time to recover from this loss [or address a health concern or take care of my family], and therefore I will be taking a one-month leave of absence. I assure you that I will be receiving the care and support I need, and I ask only that you keep my family and me in your prayers during this difficult time.* This reticence is partly to protect personal and family privacy, but it is also to avoid giving the congregation the idea that they must step in and take care of their pastor. Some congregants may ask if there is anything they can do, and there may be small practical things that would be of help. If there are, giving people an opportunity to do something positive may lessen the anxiety and sense of helplessness that beset us when someone we care about is in trouble. But this must not become an occasion to ask the congregation to reverse roles by meeting personal needs that should be addressed elsewhere.

Personal Disclosure

The question of what information to share with the community in the event of a leave of absence is a special case of a more general issue: personal disclosure. This is the matter of how much ministers should reveal about their inner personal lives and its struggles to congregants—a complicated question with no simple answer.

Part of the minister's role as a model of discipleship is to live a life with some measure of openness and transparency. It is especially important for ministers to acknowledge that human life presents challenges that Christian faith does not eliminate. While our faith assures us that God is able to redeem and make good even out of evil, Christians are not given a special exemption from hardship or suffering. Paul's declaration that "all things work together for good for those who love God" (Rom. 8:28) must be understood as expressing an ultimate viewpoint, one that sees how "suffering produces endurance, and endurance produces character, and character produces hope, and hope does not disappoint us" (Rom. 5:3–5). It is hardly a guarantee that all will be rosy along the way. Jesus promises never to forsake us, and so we may know that we do not face our trials alone. But this promise does not mean that we will never *feel* abandoned. The biblical record makes it clear that God's people experience the whole range of human emotions and experiences, and it is no lapse of faith to admit that we are struggling. Prophets and psalmists rage and lament, express terror and perplexity, and dare even to question

God in their anguish. Thus it is that Jesus himself can cry out from
the cross, "My God, my God, why have you forsaken me?" and still
be quoting Scripture (Mark 15:34; cf. Ps. 22:1).

It may be that the minister's own experiences of suffering or loss,
of felt abandonment or doubt in times of extreme challenge can serve
as invaluable testimony. They may offer a powerful witness that God
is faithful even when our faith is faltering or gone, especially if they
are shared after the storm has passed and one can look back from a
place of resolution. Such stories may also give congregants needed
permission to be truthful and secure in prayer, convinced that there is
no place to which we can be driven—either by what we do or by what
befalls us—where God will not meet us. Personal stories, therefore,
may have a place in preaching, teaching, or providing pastoral care
to those who are in crisis. As the calling to ministry embraces the
whole person, so the whole of the minister's life and faith becomes
a resource to draw on as she or he strives to lead others to a deeper
walk with God. But because risks and pitfalls can also come with this
approach, deciding what personal stories to tell—and when and how
to tell them—are matters for serious reflection and careful pastoral
judgment.

When determining whether to disclose personal information to the
congregation, there are three questions to consider. The first question
is, *Why am I choosing to share this information?* It is a natural human
impulse to reveal ourselves to people we like or to respond to personal
information shared with us by others with matching self-revelations
of our own. Such exchanges are part of building personal trust and
intimacy between friends. But this is not a sufficient or proper reason
for self-disclosure on the part of pastors, and they should not yield to
this impulse. As we have said, the nature of the pastoral relationship
is distinctive. It is not, like simple friendships, mutual, reciprocal,
and entered into on an equal footing. While pastors are there to listen to their congregants, congregants are *not* there to listen to their
pastors—at least not about their personal issues. Congregants should
not become the intimate friends and confidants of the minister, and
they should not be asked to carry the weight that often goes with
deep knowledge of another human being's soul. Instead, ministers'
conduct in such relationships must be guided by steady attention to
the congregant's needs and interests and by the demands of their

role as ministers of Jesus Christ. The first requirement, therefore, is for ministers to understand their own motives before they speak.

The second question to ask is, *What purpose do I hope telling this will serve, and is this the best way to achieve it?* In some situations ministers may share a personal story because it seems especially apt and helpful for a particular congregant or in relation to a particular topic. A minister may have a vital insight because of something she or he has gone through, or may be able to offer comfort and assurance based on having traveled the same path.[6] However, ministers must bear in mind that while they have an obligation to congregants to keep personal information confidential, congregants have no such obligation toward their ministers. The story shared with one congregant may be retold to others. It is wise, then, if ministers share only information they are willing to have known more broadly in the context of their ministry.

The third question to ask about any public self-disclosure is, *What other effects, besides the one I intend, are likely to come from sharing this story in this setting?* While there is always the possibility of an individual parishioner repeating a story to others in the community, the effect may be different if the minister shares the same story in a large-group setting, or from the pulpit. The question of setting or context is important because first-person stories are so vivid and powerful. They are likely to be remembered after other things are forgotten, including the context or conversation that prompted the disclosure. The aim of preaching should never be to draw attention to oneself, not even to one's own weakness or sinfulness; it must always be to display the goodness and power of God, and to strengthen the faith and faithfulness of the church. Therefore, the third requirement is that ministers consider whether a personal story will be a help or a distraction in proclaiming the good news.

If after answering these questions and weighing the risks, the minister's motives are clear and she or he is still persuaded that a personal story can help a congregant in trouble or give clarity and force to preaching, then there is good reason to share it. But even then, the

---

6. For instance, I have seen ministers who are themselves recovering alcoholics be of enormous assistance to others who have given up hope, or who no longer see themselves as worth saving. There is nothing quite as persuasive as the assurance, *I have been where you are now, and I promise you there is a road back.*

story should be framed so as to focus on its intended purpose, and the minister must be careful to tell it in a way that protects the privacy of any other people involved. This can be done either by remaining general in parts of the story that relate to others, or by changing enough of the setting or circumstances to preserve anonymity. When it is impossible to tell a story without revealing others' identities—such as stories that include identifiable family members—permission from these others must be received before telling the story. No one should find out during worship on Sunday morning that he or she is a sermon illustration.

There will be many times when, after careful reflection on the questions above, ministers will decide not to disclose personal information, using their experience as a source of insight and empathy but without telling their own story. Perhaps doing so would violate the privacy of others without their consent, or perhaps it simply goes too deeply into intimate personal struggles. Maybe the story would make the minister look too bad—or else too good, better than she or he actually is. Or perhaps it would simply turn the hearers' attention toward the minister and away from Jesus—a grave offense for a minister of the gospel. The heart of the matter in all such deliberations is this: Are the interests of the community well and justly served by sharing this personal information, or not?

All of us long for spaces in which anything can be said, where no topic is off limits, and where we are confident of being heard with sympathy and charity no matter what story we have to tell. Such spaces are at the heart of the deepest friendships, and a person who does not desire and cherish such profound security and trust is worse off both practically and morally. Ministers' need for relationships of this depth has already been acknowledged. But the arena of pastoral service is not the place to seek such intimacy, nor is it a place to allow such intimacy to develop even if invited by others. The ministry is the place to be present for others, and it is their well-being that must guide ministers' speech—and sometimes give reason for their silence.

One-on-One Relationships

In maintaining the boundaries that protect ministry, a particularly delicate area involves working closely with a single individual. This may occur in relation to a colleague in ministry, such as between a senior and an associate pastor, or between a pastor and a staff member. It may arise when working with a lay church leader or a member of the community on an extended project. Especially sensitive situations occur in the context of pastoral care or counseling, when a congregant seeks pastoral help to face a severe or long-term challenge. In such one-on-one contexts, all the ways in which humans form bonds with one another over shared experiences and concerns apply with special force.

One obvious risk of one-on-one relationships is the development of romantic or sexual attraction. However, there are a number of other dangers and possibilities for the relationship to become distorted as well. The formation of intense personal friendships, or relationships of excessive dependency, or even alliances that present an us-against-the-world face to other members of the community can also cause a multitude of problems, both for the two people involved and for relationships with others in the ministry setting.

Given the necessity of working with others in ministry, collaborating with lay members and staff, and offering care and counsel to those in need, it is neither practical nor desirable for pastors to avoid such risks altogether by never working one-on-one with anyone. But it is important to be thoughtful and careful about the amount of time spent with particular individuals, the duration and frequency of meetings, and the circumstances in which meetings take place.

One of the ways we send and receive messages about the nature of a conversation is by the setting in which it occurs. As we discussed in chapter 1, the contexts where ministry takes place are more flexible and variable than in the other professions, and this presents a challenge as well as a benefit. In the case of a long-term, close working relationship, such as with an associate in ministry, or an especially intense relationship, as in a pastoral counseling situation, it is wise to hold meetings in a formal work space, such as the pastor's office. The space chosen should provide the degree of privacy that is needed for the purpose of the meeting, without suggesting secrecy or the absolute privacy required for sexual intimacy. For this reason, one-on-one meetings in an otherwise empty church building are to be avoided if at all possible. Meetings can be scheduled at times when other church staff are present, or another meeting is going on next door, or the Boy Scouts are using the fellowship hall. If such times are not available, then it may be best to resort to a public space, such as a library meeting room, a coffee shop, or a local diner, to transact church business or hold a pastoral conversation.

Other social cues, such as the time of day meetings take place and the kind of clothing worn by the minister, are also significant. If possible, meetings should be held during the ordinary workday, or at a regularly scheduled evening appointment that is part of posted office or meeting hours. While in most denominational contexts a clerical collar is not necessary, attire still should be reasonably formal and conservative according to the standards of the community. It should indicate that the minister is offering a professional service, not hanging out with a friend or going on a date.

The aim of these formalities is not to multiply constraints or to create intense self-consciousness about every move a pastor makes. It is to present clear and consistent messages about what it going on here: this meeting is part of the minister's work, and she or he is there as a servant of Christ and not as a private individual looking for companionship. This does not entail that the minister's demeanor must be stiff or chilly, or that pastors ought to avoid the small talk by which we make connections with others and put them at ease. But some degree of formality reminds both the minister and the conversation partner what sort of relationship they share, and what does and does not belong in it.

In addition to providing clear communication with colleagues and congregants, exercising care and good judgment about where, when, and how to spend one-on-one time in ministry will also reduce the risk of giving others cause for worry or misunderstanding. Although the King James Version's translation of 1 Thessalonians 5:22 as "abstain from all appearance of evil" is questionable, still Christians in general and ministers in particular should not cause unnecessary anxiety to those whose intentions are good. Nor should they provide material to those who are looking for scandal. We live in a climate that seeks sensation, where trust in clergy has been greatly diminished by the revelations of misconduct that have plagued the church. We cannot take responsibility for others' suspicions, but there is no reason to add fuel to the fire. But attention to these external role markers is wasted unless care is also exercised about the content of conversation with colleagues and congregants in one-on-one meetings. This should focus on the work of the ministry or the help and counsel the pastor is there to offer. In particular, negative remarks about absent members of the community should be avoided—remarks that border on the realm of gossip instead of professional consultation—as should the kinds of inappropriate personal disclosures discussed in the previous section. Such topics are likely to confuse and distort the nature of the interaction. When a minister needs space to express irritation, to air grievances regarding work, or to talk through deep personal issues, a mentor, a senior colleague, or a wise and trusted personal friend are all more responsible choices than congregants or the colleagues you supervise in ministry.

The Usefulness of Codes—and Their Limits

Prior to the 1980s, formal and explicit statements of the ethical obligations of ministry were uncommon. Those few documents that set out moral expectations of clergy tended to be rather general and aspirational, and they focused as much on duties of professional courtesy to other ministers as on requirements and prohibitions in relation to congregants. Today codes of ethics for ministers are readily available in the literature on ethics and the practice of ministry and in the training and disciplinary materials of various Protestant denominations.[7] These offer some variety in explicit expectations and instructions and differ somewhat in the topics they take up. But they have several things in common, including addressing certain minimal requirements of integrity in pastoral service to the community. Ministers who are regular employees of the church are commonly adjured to devote themselves full time to their pastoral service, to perform their pastoral duties without seeking additional compensation, and to treat members of the parish respectfully and without partiality. They are encouraged to maintain regular habits of study and personal devotion as part of fitness for their work, and to behave in a collegial and supportive manner to clergy colleagues.

7. In *Ministerial Ethics: Moral Formation for Church Leaders*, 2nd ed. (Grand Rapids: Baker Academic, 2004), Joe E. Trull and James E. Carter offer a particularly helpful chapter on the topic, along with appendices offering several examples.

Notably, ethical codes written in the last few decades are more careful and detailed in naming obligations to maintain the confidences of congregants, to exercise careful stewardship and reporting in financial matters, and to refrain from any sexual involvement with members of the community served, as in these examples:

> I will under no circumstances violate confidences that come to me as a minister.[8]
>
> I will be honest in my stewardship of money.[9]
>
> I will not invade the private and intimate bonds of others' lives, nor will I trespass on those bonds for my own advantage or need when they are disturbed.[10]
>
> I will not exploit the needs of another person to meet my own.[11]
>
> I will not engage in sexual activity with a member of the congregation who is not my spouse or partner.[12]

Perhaps the most broadly conceived and ample statement on abuse of authority is the covenant found in the Code of Ethics for Ordained and Licensed Ministers in the Church of the Brethren:

> We will not misuse the trust that is placed in us and the unique power inherent in our function by exploiting in any way those who seek our help and care. We will guard against violating the emotional, physical and spiritual well-being of people who come to us for help or over whom we have any kind of authority. We will not use that authority to defame, manipulate either individual or congregational decisions, or to create dependencies. We will avoid situations or relationships which could impair our professional judgment, compromise the integrity of our ministry, or use the situation or relationship for our own gain. We will avoid all sexual exploitation or harassment in professional or social relationships, even when others invite such behavior or involvement.[13]

8. The Disciples' Code of Ethics.
9. Ibid.
10. Code of Professional Practices, Unitarian Universalist Ministers' Association, June 1988.
11. Ibid.
12. Ibid.
13. Quoted in Trull and Carter, *Ministerial Ethics*, 238.

I have already made a case for how explicit statements of this kind, which spell out what is required and what is out of bounds in ministry, are valuable and helpful. Simply rehearsing such obligations raises one's level of awareness and attention, and helps to create a climate in which violations are more likely to be reported. In addition, making promises in public can strengthen one's resolve to keep them when it becomes hard to do so. This is vital because over a lifetime in ministry a pastor's obligations may become difficult, even painfully difficult, to fulfill. Others' secrets may come to seem burdensome and unworthy of protection. Financial propriety may yield to anxiety and strain about how to make ends meet on a modest salary. Feelings of loneliness or unjust criticism may make the grateful congregant or counselee a tempting source of personal affirmation. In these moments of weakness or temptation, a public commitment to maintaining boundaries in ministry can serve as an important reminder and support.

At the same time, most pastoral misconduct is not the result of fully conscious choices, entered into as the result of reasoned deliberation about what would be best for oneself and others. Pastoral violations commonly arise under pressure, in a sea of half-understood feelings and motivations and in a moment of temporary suspension of clarity and judgment. And once the line is crossed, impulsively or out of desperation, matters are further confused by fear, guilt, self-doubt, and self-justification until it is difficult to think at all—hard to see clearly where choices have led, and harder still to find a road back. These observations are not intended to minimize or excuse the misconduct of ministers, which is grave indeed. They serve merely to highlight the circumstances in which most of the pastors who end up doing wrong go astray, even if their initial intentions were good.

Thus, while it is valuable and even indispensable to have clear rules, requirements, and prohibitions in place, these serve more like guardrails on the highway than like a roadmap to fidelity: by the time you run into one, you are already in trouble. For this reason, it is vital for pastors who hope to remain faithful over decades of professional service to learn to pay close attention to themselves and to those they serve. They must be keenly aware of their own vulnerabilities and those of other people, attuned to the fears, losses, and challenges in life that can make any of us liable to fall. The pastor who is navigating a painful conflict in the church is likely to seek supportive allies—and perhaps to break confidences in the process. Expectations of scrupulous integrity in the handling of church funds may never have given a pastor pause—until the car needs an expensive repair and the first tuition bill comes due. The congregant who seeks counsel about a deeply unhappy marriage will be sorely tempted to look for comfort and affirmation from the minister—and they are both at risk should the pastor's emotional needs happen to intersect with the parishioner's.

Codes of conduct, however well-conceived, do not make anyone immune to temptation, nor do they provide foolproof protection against moral failure. Unfortunately, little attention is given in formation for ministry to the high likelihood of serious moral struggles arising in the course of years of pastoral service, or to developing strategies for responding to them. Many beginning ministers enter into their work with no idea that the ethical obligations they so readily assented to in seminary might take real discipline and genuine sacrifice to meet. But moral maturity does not consist in being incorruptible. It consists in knowing one's weaknesses and in being alert to the first signs of breakdown in the boundaries that protect ministry. It requires having in place the spiritual and interpersonal resources to respond to such intimations of risk, and having the courage and clarity of heart to call on those resources in time.

In chapter 5 we turn to the essential spiritual disciplines that undergird life in ministry by developing the kind of maturity and spiritual depth that can sustain faithfulness in times of challenge. But before turning to those disciplines, it is necessary to delve more deeply into why and how ministers—including those who care profoundly about their work and are most personally invested in it—can get themselves in moral trouble. In chapter 4, I examine the underlying dynamics that make ministry a more common arena for misconduct (particularly sexual misconduct) than the other professions, in the hope that greater insight will offer greater protection. I also offer practical guidance for recognizing and responding to signs of danger if they arise.

4

Understanding How Ministers Get into Trouble

The ongoing series of sex scandals that have rocked the church in America and abroad since the 1980s have left many observers stunned and bewildered. These scandals have toppled prominent leaders and devastated communities across a range of denominations— from Catholic to Mennonite, from Southern Baptist to Unitarian Universalist—and it seems that no group is exempt. The child sex abuse crisis in the American Catholic Church, brought to public attention by the media in 2002, may be the best known and most alarming of these scandals in the US. But perhaps a more common form of misconduct is that of boundary violations in which ministers become sexually involved with other adults whom they serve as pastors, see as counselors, or supervise in ministry. Both individual case studies and social scientific surveys make clear that this problem is more prevalent than anyone suspected.[1] The general public is rightly

1. Diana R. Garland and Christen Argueta note a variation in percentages of clergy self-reporting sexual misconduct from 1 percent to 15 percent ("How Clergy Sexual Misconduct Happens: A Qualitative Study of First-Hand Accounts," *Social Work and Christianity* 37 [2010]: 4), while Katheryn A. Flynn cites other sources that claim self-reporting percentages as high as 38.6 percent for "inappropriate sexual contact" (*The Sexual Abuse of Women by Members of the Clergy* [Jefferson, NC: McFarland, 2003], 3).

outraged, and even many of the faithful are severely disillusioned. Trust in ministers has fallen dramatically in the past few decades, and some have left the church altogether over this issue.[2]

Ministers are not the only professionals who abuse positions of power, violate professional obligations, and exploit the trust of those placed in their care. Doctors have knowingly performed unnecessary procedures on patients for profit, therapists have taken advantage of the emotional vulnerability of those they counsel for personal gratification, and attorneys have misused clients' funds or confidential information to benefit themselves. Members of these professions have also been found guilty of sexual violations, including rape and child molestation. But there is something uniquely awful about a minister—someone who is entrusted with the spiritual welfare of others, whose office endows her or him with sacred authority, and whose public workspace is called a "sanctuary"—using that position to take sexual advantage of those in her or his care.

Therefore, the most disturbing news of all may be that sexual misconduct is *more* common among clergy than among other professionals—a conclusion based on self-reporting by ministers as well as on the accounts of those who tally reported violations by all categories of professionals.[3] These studies suggest that ministers are more likely than other professionals to cross boundaries and become

2. See Michael Lipka, "Why America's 'Nones' Left Religion Behind," Pew Research Center, August 24, 2016, http://www.pewresearch.org/fact-tank/2016/08/24/why-americas-nones-left-religion-behind/. This is especially often reported by young people. See, e.g., Brandon Vogt, *Return: How to Draw Your Child Back to the Church* (Winter Spring, FL: Numinous, 2015).

3. For instance, a denominational panel of the United Church of Canada found in 1992 that "clergy are sexually exploiting parishioners at twice the rate of secular therapists" (cited in Stanley J. Grenz and Roy D. Bell, *Betrayal of Trust: Confronting and Preventing Clergy Sexual Misconduct*, 2nd ed. [Grand Rapids: Baker Books, 2001], 22). However, all such comparative estimates depend upon a combination of self-reporting surveys and the processing of formal complaints against professionals in various fields. These are difficult to compare because of situational variables and differences in definitions and statistical methods. As we noted in the introduction, Pamela Cooper-White estimates, "Somewhere between one in eight and one in three clergy have crossed sexual boundaries with their parishioners" (*The Cry of Tamar: Violence against Women and the Church's Response* [Minneapolis: Fortress, 1995], 149), whereas Randy Sansone and Lori Sansone report that just under 7 percent of US physicians self-report sexual contact with present patients ("Crossing the Line: Sexual Boundary Violations by Physicians," *Psychiatry* 6 [June 2009]: 45–48).

sexually involved with those they pastor or counsel. Some see this as proof that organized religion is a fraud. Whether or not there is a God, they claim, we shouldn't trust anyone who claims to represent God, and the institutional church exists chiefly to serve its leaders.[4] But even those who are profoundly cynical about the church do not provide an explanation for why ministers in particular seem liable to misuse professional authority in this way.

Even prior to the scandals of recent years, the decline in the centrality of the church in American life has meant that clergy are no longer among the most highly esteemed members of our society. Neither are they the most highly educated nor the most highly paid. In general, the prestige that goes with the ministry today is less than that attached to the professions of medicine and law. Based on a calculation of required preparation versus expected income, or hours and intensity of work versus the social and material rewards offered over time, it hardly makes sense to become a minister as a strategy for pursuing the perquisites of power.[5] Although we rightly identify the heart of pastoral misconduct as an abuse of power rather than simply a matter of succumbing to lust or romantic passion, it still seems unlikely that those who are primarily motivated by power-seeking are disproportionately drawn to ministry as a profession. There must be another explanation for why so many of those who enter pastoral work fall into such a grave and obvious corruption of their office.

Part of the answer is suggested by the distinctive aspects of the profession of ministry noted in chapter 1. There is the complex and multilayered character of relationships between ministers and congregants. There is ministry's relative lack of the contextual role-markers supplied by a unique location of service and well-defined external structures—markers that reinforce the nature of the relationship

---

4. For instance, see James Hervey Johnson, "God Is a Myth and Religion Is a Gigantic Fraud," Church and State, http://churchandstate.org.uk/2017/01/god-is-a-myth-and-religion-is-a-gigantic-fraud/.

5. It is imaginable that a sexual predator might intentionally seek such a career in order to exploit the access it gives to vulnerable people. However, research uniformly indicates the great majority of boundary violators among the clergy fall into the category of "wanderers," those who start with good intentions and slide by degrees into wrongdoing. See Marie M. Fortune, *Is Nothing Sacred? When Sex Invades the Pastoral Relationship* (San Francisco: HarperSanFrancisco, 1989), 156n1; Grenz and Bell, *Betrayal of Trust*, 42–44.

between lawyers and their clients and between doctors and their patients. Finally, there is the deeply personal character of pastoral power, including being entrusted with confidential information and sharing the most intense and vulnerable moments in people's lives. Clearly such factors can contribute to the blurring of roles on both sides, as well as increasing the practical opportunity for sexual boundary violations. But I want to suggest another element that accounts for the prevalence of sexual misconduct among clergy, one that is more incalculable and harder to control. This is the deep connection that exists in human beings between sexuality and spirituality. This claim may seem strange and surprising to some, but the signs of it are everywhere, beginning in Scripture.

Sexuality and Spirituality in Scripture and Tradition

The ancient biblical writers sought to draw the sharpest possible contrast between devotion to the God of the covenant and participation in the fertility cults of the surrounding Canaanite cultures. The prophets rail against the worship of Baal and his female consort Ashtoreth,[6] worship that involved orgiastic celebrations and ritual prostitution. They fiercely reject the commonplace cosmology of the time—wherein god and goddess together give birth to the world—and insist on complete loyalty to the Holy One of Israel, the Creator who rules alone and has no consort. Thus it might be surprising that the bond between God and the covenant people is recurrently rendered in Hebrew Scripture in the language of erotic love and marriage.

A few of many examples illustrate the point. Through the prophet Jeremiah, God tells his people: "I remember the devotion of your youth, your love as a bride, how you followed me in the wilderness, in a land not sown. Israel was holy to the LORD, the first fruits of his harvest" (Jer. 2:2–3). Just as the fruition of the covenant is spoken of as a marriage, so departure from its bonds in pursuit of other gods is portrayed as adultery and culminates in divorce. Alluding to the hilltop shrines and sacred trees of pagan worship, Jeremiah again

---

6. One of a number of variant spellings occurring in Hebrew Scripture for the Babylonian goddess who is Baal's counterpart, called Astarte by the Greeks. Cf. Judges 2:13; 1 Samuel 7:4, 12:10.

speaks for God: "Have you seen what [Israel] did, . . . how she went up on every high hill and under every green tree, and played the whore there? . . . [Judah] saw that for all the adulteries of that faithless one, Israel, I had sent her away with a decree of divorce; yet her false sister Judah did not fear, but she too went and played the whore" (Jer. 3:6–8). But God's anger cannot endure forever, and when it abates and Israel is pardoned, the restoration of God's people is depicted by the prophet Hosea as a purified and restored marriage covenant: "I will take you for my wife forever; I will take you for my wife in righteousness and in justice, in steadfast love, and in mercy. I will take you for my wife in faithfulness; and you shall know the LORD" (Hos. 2:19–20). Isaiah invokes the same language to declare God's forgiving mercy after exile: "For your Maker is your husband. . . . The LORD has called you like a wife forsaken and grieved in spirit, like the wife of a man's youth when she is cast off. . . . For a brief moment I abandoned you, but with great compassion I will gather you" (Isa. 54: 5–7). And perhaps the most striking example of all is the inclusion of the Song of Songs in the canon of Hebrew Scripture. Whatever the writer's original intention, this book gives testimony to the power and antiquity of erotic love as a symbol of the passionate attachment between God and Israel.

The analogy to the Lord as husband and God's people as wife continues in the New Testament. John the Baptist likens Christ to the bridegroom to whom the bride belongs, the one at whose coming John, as the groom's friend, rejoices (John 3:29). Jesus repeatedly draws on the motif of marriage in parables of the kingdom (Matt. 22:1–14; Luke 14:7–14), and he answers the question about why his disciples do not fast by saying that the wedding guests do not fast while the bridegroom is among them (Mark 2:19). The same theme reappears in Ephesians 5, where husbands are enjoined to love their wives as Christ loved the church, giving himself up to make her holy and cherishing her as his own body (5:25–30). The writer of Ephesians then borrows from Genesis the language of marriage making husband and wife "one flesh" and declares that this is a "great mystery" that applies to Christ and the church (5:31–32). In Revelation, the celebration of the salvation wrought by God through Christ is depicted as a wedding feast: "'Let us rejoice and exult and give him the glory, for the marriage of the Lamb has come, and his bride has

made herself ready; to her it has been granted to be clothed with
fine linen, bright and pure'—for the fine linen is the righteous deeds
of the saints" (19:7–8). The climax of the vision comes with the de-
scent of the new Jerusalem, the city of peace, coming down out of
heaven "as a bride adorned for her husband" (21:2). An angel leads
the visionary to view the holy city, lavished with gates of jewels and
streets of gold, saying, "Come, I will show you the bride, the wife
of the Lamb" (21:9).

The theme of the Lord being joined as in marriage to God's people
is taken up and richly developed throughout subsequent Christian
tradition. In early Christian texts the church collectively is called the
bride of Christ. By the beginning of the monastic period, individual
believers (particularly those belonging to religious orders) are spoken
of as "betrothed" or "wedded" to Christ.[7] The idea of a marriage between Christ and church is already taken for granted in the undivided
church by the fourth century, present in sermons and catechetical texts
as diverse as Augustine's commentary on the Psalms and Cyril of
Jerusalem's series of sermons instructing new believers in the faith.[8]
The same motif is woven into the prayers and chants of the liturgy,
a pattern that continues in both East and West after the schism. For
instance, the prescribed service for Tuesday morning of Holy Week in
the Orthodox Church is called the "Bridegroom Matins" and features
prayers like the following: "Let us love the Bridegroom, O Brethren.
Let us keep our lamps aflame with virtues and true faith, so that we,
like the wise virgins of the Lord, may be ready to enter with Him
into the marriage feast. For the Bridegroom, as God, grants unto all
an incorruptible crown."[9]

7. See Morwenna Ludlow, *The Early Church* (New York: Tauris, 2007), 77–78.
For a rich and detailed accounting of this metaphor in the lives of women religious,
consult Rabia Gregory, "Marrying Jesus: Brides and the Bridegroom in Medieval
Women's Religious Literature," PhD diss., University of North Carolina at Chapel
Hill, 2007, https://cdr.lib.unc.edu/indexablecontent/uuid:dbcaac3a-c91e-4eb3-bb18
-852a84d09859.
8. E.g., Cyril of Jerusalem, "Catechetical Lectures," trans. Edwin Hamilton Gif-
ford, in *Nicene and Post-Nicene Fathers: Second Series*, vol. 7, ed. Philip Schaff and
Henry Wace (Buffalo, NY: Christian Literature Publishing, 1894); Augustine of Hippo,
"Exposition on Psalm 127," trans. J. E. Tweed, in *Nicene and Post-Nicene Fathers: First
Series*, vol. 8, ed. Philip Schaff (Buffalo, NY: Christian Literature Publishing, 1888).
9. Hugh Wybrew, *Orthodox Lent, Holy Week and Easter: Liturgical Texts with
Commentary* (Crestwood, NY: St. Vladimir Seminary Press, 1977), 93.

In spiritual and devotional works, the language of erotic love has regularly been used to speak of the passion of the soul for God, and the biblical command to "love the LORD your God with all your heart, and with all your soul, and with all your might" (Deut. 6:5; cf. Matt. 22:37; Mark 12:30; Luke 10: 27) has been expounded as the requirement that God be first in our hearts, as the bride forsakes all others to cleave to her husband alone. Medieval classics of religious life such as Saint Bernard of Clairvaux's commentary on the Song of Songs develop this theme into a full-blown allegory. Bernard interprets the Song of Songs as a guide to mystical ascent toward union with Christ through ascetical practice and contemplative prayer. He appropriates the erotic language without embarrassment, as the bride's desire to kiss the feet, the hands, and finally the mouth of her lover is expounded as the steps of repentance, growth in devotion through prayer, and finally the full bliss of union with the Bridegroom.[10]

The use of language that evokes romantic and marital love to convey the love between God and humankind is not limited to ancient texts. Both traditional and contemporary hymns do the same thing. From Charles Wesley's classic "Jesus, Lover of My Soul," to the romanticism of C. Austin Miles's "In the Garden (I Come to the Garden Alone)," to Michael W. Smith's ballad-like contemporary chorus "Draw Me Close," writers and poets reach for language that can express the depth and power of God's love for humankind, and the passionate longing of the believer to be filled with that divine love. It is no wonder that they often find such language in one of the most overwhelming and intense forms of human love, the love that involves being taken out of ourselves and freed from the reach of calculation and self-interest through profound identification with another person. As C. S. Lewis observes in *The Four Loves*, falling in love offers us a kind of foretaste of one of the highest fruits of holy

---

10. See Bernard of Clairvaux, *On the Song of Songs I*, trans. Kilian Walsh (Kalamazoo, MI: Cistercian, 1970); *On the Song of Songs II*, trans. Kilian Walsh (Kalamazoo, MI: Cistercian 1976); *On the Song of Songs III*, trans. Kilian Walsh and Irene Edmonds (Kalamazoo, MI: Cistercian, 1979); *On the Song of Songs IV*, trans. Irene Edmonds (Kalamazoo, MI: Cistercian, 1980). For a general summary of the prevalence and interpretation of erotic imagery, see Matthew Milliner, "Sex and Mysticism," *First Things*, September 19, 2007, https://www.firstthings.com/web-exclusives/2007/09/sex-and-mysticism.

charity: the capacity for self-forgetfulness in complete devotion to another.[11]

But there is more to the connection between spiritual life and sexual love than reaching for metaphors to convey the intensity and depth of a desire for God, or the passionate nature of God's love for humankind. There is also the fact that many of the things we look for in religious life we also hope and long for in romantic and sexual relationships. These longings correspond to our deepest joys and our keenest vulnerabilities as human beings. We thus need to examine more closely how they relate to one another in the context of ministry, beginning with the desires that draw us into religious life and community.

Sexuality and Spirituality in Ministry

At the deepest level, we come to church looking to be recognized, called by name and received as a unique individual. We seek a relationship with God because we want to be known fully and truthfully, all the way down, and yet still to be loved. We search for a space in which it is safe to let down our guard, a place where we can drop our pretenses and admit our failures and neediness without fear of being ridiculed, judged, or abandoned. We long for someone to whom we can tell the whole truth—even the secrets we attempt to keep from ourselves. We hope to find someone who can help us to face who we are, and also give us the power to become different and better than we are. Ultimately, we seek the One who will receive and welcome us, no matter what, and from whom we need not hide. If we have heard the gospel message aright, understood the stories about lost sheep and lost sons and daughters, then it is just possible that God is indeed the One before whom all may be brought without dissembling, and the church a place where this welcoming God might be encountered and made real to us. A congregation that knows it lives entirely on God's mercy, and one that can make this mercy and welcome visible, has a life-giving ministry to offer.

But wisely or not, successfully or not, in hope or in desperation, we also seek to meet many of these same deep human needs in intimate relationship with another person. In sexual relationships in

11. C. S. Lewis, *The Four Loves* (New York: Harcourt, Brace, 1960), 158–59.

particular, we seek a chance to escape our isolation and lay down our fears, to be known in truth and cherished all the same. We seek someone with whom we can be naked and unashamed, hoping for a remembrance of life in the Garden before evil tainted the sweetest of God's gifts: the companionship in mind, body, and spirit of one who is flesh of our flesh. We want someone who delights in us and whom we can delight in. We long for the physical union that can lift for a moment the burden of separateness that comes with being alive in a body. In the same way that romantic love can be a foretaste of holy charity, then, sex at its best can offer a foretaste of the perfectly trusting communion with another person for which we long.

It is vital to remember that God has made humans this way on purpose, God who made sex to be life-giving far beyond the biology of reproduction, instilling into each of us the longing to be made "one flesh" with another human being. Human sexuality is part of the divine strategy for pulling us out of ourselves and into relationship, away from the death of isolation and toward life and flourishing. Our desire for physical and emotional union with another person is a mark of our creation in the image of God, whose being is the divine community of the Trinity. The same taproot of desire for intimacy and connection, for perfect safety and utter entrustment, runs through both religion and sexuality. It is what gives sex its capacity to join hearts and souls as well as bodies, and what gives potency and passion to religion.

It is thus no accident that, as we saw above, the metaphor of marriage runs through Scripture, or that the mystics so often speak of God as the great Lover. The current that connects religion and human desire for intimacy is God's idea, and so we must affirm that it is good. But we must recognize that it is also dangerous, especially in the context of ministry. We are all liable to mistake the intoxication of romance for the attainment of true charity, and we are often ready to substitute sexual union for the fuller and freer communion of souls united by devotion to God. Even when our intentions are good, it is not hard to see how these overlapping constellations of things we long for could be mistaken for one another: how they might become commingled and confused in our minds and imaginations so that we go looking for one set of profound human needs to be met in a place that is fitted only to address the other.

In the context of ministry, all this is more than academic. The
work of a pastor is to make the good news of God's mercy not only
heard but also seen, not only understood but also made present, be-
lievable, and lovable. This work requires all the gifts and graces God
has bestowed on those who serve the gospel—everything learned in
school, all the information and skills acquired from books, mentors,
and experience in ministry. But it also draws upon the full range of
the minister's humanity: personal charm, warmth, care, competence,
humor, sensitivity, intelligence, and even the deep current of his or
her life as an embodied and sexual being. There is no other way to
be present in ministry than as a whole human being, one with all
the dimensions of human personality and all the needs and vulnerabilities that go with them. Even with all the precautions discussed
in chapter 3 in place, there is no way to enter into this life of service
without daring a genuine personal presence, for it is a necessary condition of effective preaching, teaching, counseling, and care-giving.
But this means that it is easier than one might think for ministers to
slide from leading others to a deeper trust in God to leading them to
depend on the minister personally: easier to turn from offering them
Christ as the ultimate Friend and Lover to offering oneself, almost
without noticing that this is what one has begun to do. And a person
does not have to go very far down that road before it is extremely
hard to turn back.

This is the reason for insisting that ministers must give careful, regular attention to their own needs for rest and respite, for
friendship, laughter, and personal intimacy as a means of sustaining faithfulness in ministry. It is also the reason for cultivating deep
self-awareness and awareness of others, and for keeping in place
the structures and guidelines that protect ministers and congregants
from the confusion and self-deception that lead into wrongdoing.
But even with wise and humble self-care and thoughtfully drawn
boundaries in place, no one should suppose he or she is proof against
blindness or immune to temptation. Everyone is susceptible to falling, as the saints of Christian history would be the first to tell us.
Ministers must therefore be vigilant in guarding themselves from
the kinds of moral distortions that occur when they seek to meet
their good and normal human needs for intimacy through their
pastoral service.

Guarding Ministry from Sexual Misconduct

In chapter 2 we discussed how healthy practices of physical, emotional, and spiritual self-care go far to keep a minister from being overwhelmed by unmet personal needs. And in chapter 3 we added that clear and consistent behavioral messages about the nature and purposes of pastoral relationships help forestall confusion about what kind of needs can legitimately be met in the context of ministry. But with the rate of sexual misconduct among clergy so high, and the consequences so grave, there are still other precautions to take. First, ministers need to be aware of the interpersonal dynamics that operate in pastoral ministry, especially in pastoral counseling, and how they contribute to risk. Second, they must be mindful of times when they are especially vulnerable, exercising particular caution at those times. Third, they should always be on the alert for practical signs that indicate they might be in danger. Finally, they must think concretely in advance about what to do if they find themselves in trouble—for instance, actively and seriously attracted to a congregant, or suddenly aware of being invited by a counselee into a sexual relationship that it would be a betrayal of their ministerial office to enter. Below we address each of these additional safeguards in turn.

Recognizing the Dynamics of Care

No matter what the particular setting, all pastoral ministry depends on forming relationships. From this foundation follow all the elements on which human connections are based, everything that makes spiritual leadership and caregiving possible. But these same elements can be subject to misinterpretation or deflection, to the point that what is undertaken as a responsible pastoral relationship becomes distorted in the minds of the participants. From there it is but a small step to actual misconduct. To safeguard against such distortion, it is helpful to review the dynamics of ministry—particularly of counseling and pastoral care—and the emotions that can arise in its course. This allows us to consider more carefully the risks that accompany such services. To be sure, pastoral care is not the only arena in which relationships can become distorted and boundaries breached, but it nevertheless provides a useful lens through which to consider these dynamics. Here we consider the elements of time, trust, identification and empathy, and transference and countertransference that are key aspects of effective pastoral counseling.

TIME

Becoming someone's pastor takes time. Although it is possible for a minister to drive in from a distance and lead a liturgy or deliver a sermon, to drop in at the hospital or show up for a committee meeting, anyone who has ever been a minister knows that this is not enough to make one a pastor. Effectiveness in any of these activities is based on the time already invested in the community and its members: the conversations, shared experiences, and common work and play that build a connection so that leadership can be trusted, preaching heard, and visits welcomed. There is no substitute for taking the time to be present. This is particularly vital in relation to offering pastoral care and counsel, but here it is also a matter for special caution. As we noted in chapter 3, with extended one-on-one time comes increased emotional attachment and the risk of dependency, especially for a congregant who is confronting great challenges. For this reason, pastors should confine sessions with individuals to relatively brief periods. (Therapists' standard fifty-minute "hour" is not a bad model.) In addition, ministers should not undertake counseling of extended duration unless they have both relevant special training and a structured institutional context to do so. Otherwise, pastors should maintain a list of local counselors in various specialties whose credentials and competence they have investigated, and they should refer parishioners in need of extended counseling to these professionals, while continuing in a secondary, supportive role.

TRUST

Part of the need for time in building pastoral relationships is to establish trust. This includes confidence in the minister's knowledge and skill, and that he or she will use those abilities reliably for the benefit of the congregant. Without such confidence, no effective spiritual guidance or care can be offered. Thus, to do their work well ministers must cultivate the trust of those they serve. But with such trust comes a profound responsibility. It is altogether too easy to misuse trust, to let the sense of being relied on and confided in feed one's need for importance and admiration rather than driving one more deeply into thoughtful reflection and prayer. Such a deflection already shifts the pastoral relationship, turning it away from the congregant's needs and toward the minister's. At the extreme, the interpersonal power that is based on trust can become a weapon against the vulnerable. A common element in the most egregious and devastating cases of pastoral misconduct is the exploitation of the congregant's trust in the wisdom and unselfishness of the one posing as shepherd, trust that keeps the victim from identifying the abuse or withdrawing from the relationship even when suffering greatly.

IDENTIFICATION AND EMPATHY

In order to help those in confusion or trouble, ministers must establish a bond with them based on the commonalities that all people share. There must be a measure of identification with counselees or congregants, a way to enter into their experience and understand their behavior to some degree, even if part of the work to be done is to find new and healthier ways to respond in the future. Without such a connection, it is difficult to find insight into another person and give useful guidance, and it is hard for the congregant to receive it. Empathy is an essential tool, making space for the safe disclosure of difficult or embarrassing information, and helping to sustain the pastoral relationship through the challenges that may come with offering spiritual guidance. (Indeed, a pastor who can find no point of identification and no ground of empathy with someone who comes for care may be best advised to refer that person to another pastor or counselor right away.)

At the same time, the potency of emotional identification also makes it a source of possible danger, particularly if the pastoral caregiver becomes so identified with the congregant that the pastor takes on the congregant's problems as his or her own to solve. This not only invades the realm of ultimate freedom and responsibility that belongs to every adult human; it also can cause the would-be caregiver to lose perspective and cross boundaries in an effort to find—or to be—the solution. This is especially likely when the issues are serious, such as chronic infidelity or abuse within an intimate relationship.

Pastors' frustration with the limits of what they can do in such a situation may lead them to believe that this case is an exception, and that since abiding by the rules will not solve the problem, the rules must not apply. But such thoughts should serve as warning signals of potential trouble—all the more reason to keep the appropriate boundaries in place.

TRANSFERENCE AND COUNTER-TRANSFERENCE

The investment of time, the establishment of trust, and the development of identification and empathy between the pastor and congregant—including the resultant sense of frustration when problems seem intractable—are routine elements of any kind of helping relationship, present to some extent whenever we seek or offer professional assistance. Like all forms of interpersonal power, their potential to do good also entails their capacity to be misdirected and do harm. This is the reason for returning again and again to the paired protections of disciplined self-care and well-defined professional boundaries. But in the particular case of individual pastoral counseling, another powerful set of forces can be at work, the phenomena called transference and counter-transference.

In its most general sense, transference is taking feelings that originate in one relationship and unconsciously redirecting them into another relationship. This can be as simple as being inclined to like someone who resembles a good friend or, conversely, to distrust a person whose appearance or manner reminds us of someone who has harmed us in the past. Some degree of transference is routine in human interaction, and it subtly shapes how we perceive and react to other people all the time. But a special instance of this unconscious emotional transfer between disparate relationships often develops during a therapeutic process. It can be a way of working out in a safer and more structured space feelings and issues that are unresolved, whether from a person's past or from a current troubled relationship. Psychiatrists and psychotherapists are trained to identify and use such psychological dynamics as ways to illuminate underlying issues, and thus to help in diagnosis and treatment. They are also taught to recognize them for what they are: displaced patterns of relating that do not have to do with the professional caregiver but with other people in the client's life.

This recognition is important, because transference does not operate in a vacuum. Being on the receiving end of someone else's projected emotions—whether anger or affection, suspicion or desire—naturally triggers emotional responses in the counselor as well, the secondary layer of projection called counter-transference. It requires skill, discipline, and support to properly identify one's own reactions and to manage them appropriately so that the therapeutic relationship can remain a safe and protected space for healing. The lack of specialized training and the absence of an institutional context for support and supervision for the pastoral caregiver are major reasons that pastors without these resources are cautioned against entering into prolonged or profound engagements in pastoral counseling. Without such clinical training and supervision, the potent interpersonal dynamics of therapy are too dangerous and are thus best avoided.

Being Mindful of Vulnerability

No one lives a life free of challenges. All ministers face periods in which their personal lives are more painful than rewarding, or when the obligations of pastoral work are laid on top of a crisis within their own families. If the pastor is also a parent, then even ordinary demands like caring for a new baby or negotiating the tensions that come with the emergence of an adolescent into greater independence can cause considerable strain. As discussed in chapter 3, some of these occasions may rise to the level of requiring professional help or a leave of absence from active ministry. But usually they fall within the range of the normal ups and downs that we all must weather. Still, a minister is wise to be aware of the ways in which challenges in other aspects of life may increase his or her vulnerability to confusion or temptation, and to take special care in observing good boundaries between personal needs and professional responsibilities. The following are some of the routine conditions that contribute to risk and call for closer monitoring.

FATIGUE

Anyone who has ever lost his temper at the end of a long workday, or said something she instantly regretted in a meeting that ran past nine at night, knows that being tired decreases one's grip on emotions and impairs one's judgment. For this reason, pastors who know they are fatigued need to exercise particular care. Whatever the cause—whether worn out from an intense period at work, sleep-deprived because of a new infant in the household, or just entering a fourth meeting of the afternoon—a pastor who is fatigued is operating without a normal degree of reflectivity and self-control, and thus is liable to act more impulsively and with fewer inhibitions. It is a state that calls for heightened vigilance.

Loneliness

Although pastoring requires a great deal of interaction with other people, it can still be quite lonely at times. The pastor leads and guides a community but is never fully a member of that community. Pastors may like and even grow to love the people for whom they care, but congregants are not their peers and cannot be their support system. At the same time, the demands of ministry are such that it is difficult to maintain a work schedule that corresponds to other people's hours, and so it is hard to find regular time to spend with friends outside the congregation. And even during times with close friends, there are often problems a pastor cannot talk about and burdens a pastor cannot share. It is not uncommon for pastors to feel isolated or to feel that no one understands what their experience is like. Such feelings are normal, but they also constitute risk factors, making one more likely to share information or seek companionship in a way that crosses boundaries. When aware of feelings of loneliness, the pastor should reach out to a partner or trusted friend, even if it must be by telephone, to talk through these feelings and what will help.

Frustration

The work of ministry is often hard. Many times the pastor's best efforts are thwarted: when unhealthy patterns of church life seem impossible to change, when vital programs wither for lack of support, when people suffering the effects of unwise choices seem unable to keep from repeating them, or when all the labor and passion poured into preaching and teaching seem to go for nothing because no one is listening. It can be hard to remember that half the work of leadership consists in hanging in there, continuing to offer a vision of hope for what God can yet do in a community or a life. Intense frustration may indicate the need for the pastor to find a way to recharge and recapture personal confidence and trust that God has not finished with him or her and the congregation. This might be a personal retreat or an engaging conference for ministers or a few days away with colleagues to share ideas and encouragement. But in the meantime, the pastor must remember that frustration increases the chances of crossing lines in pursuit of some good end, and so must exercise particular care.

CONFLICT

Conflict is a common enough feature of human interactions to have spawned a wealth of literature. Many social scientific studies analyze patterns of responding to conflict along axes such as assertiveness versus accommodation or engagement versus withdrawal.[12] A wealth of popular material examines different strategies for managing conflict and offers advice about how to address it, including a number of books aimed specifically at church leaders.[13] But the point here is more general: the circumstance of conflict within the church, whether ideological or interpersonal, creates additional stress for the minister, contributing another possible source of moral vulnerability. The same is true of conflict within a pastor's household. Whenever a person feels under attack or feels that the safe haven she or he has labored to create in the church or the home has broken down, it is natural to look for allies. The sense of being embattled increases the chance of boundary violations, for which pastors must be alert.

MARITAL DIFFICULTIES

What is true of any conflict in the home is especially true of prolonged and serious conflict or alienation between a pastor and his or

---

12. E.g., Lourdes Munduate, Juan Ganaza, José M. Peiró, and Martin Euwema, "Patterns of Styles in Conflict Management and Effectiveness," *International Journal of Conflict Management* 10 (1999): 5–24; Robert J. Sternberg and Diane M. Dobson, "Resolving Interpersonal Conflicts: An Analysis of Stylistic Consistency," *Journal of Personality and Social Psychology* 52 (1987): 794–812.

13. For instance, Kenneth O. Gangrel and Sam Canine, *Communication and Conflict Management in Churches and Christian Organizations* (Eugene, OR: Wipf and Stock, 2002); Deborah van Deusen Hunsinger and Theresa F. Latini, *Transforming Church Conflict: Compassionate Leadership in Action* (Louisville: Westminster John Knox, 2013); David W. Kale, *Managing Conflict in the Church* (Kansas City, MO: Beacon Hill, 2003).

her partner. The disruption of a person's primary emotional support system is painful and destabilizing. Ministers facing significant marital difficulties must regard themselves as acutely vulnerable and seek help and support not only for the sake of their marriage, but for the sake of the community they are charged to shepherd. They should not suppose that because they are able to offer helpful counsel regarding others' marriages, they do not need a marital counselor themselves! The old adage about a lawyer who represents himself in court having a fool for a client applies also to pastoral care and counseling. If they are not being addressed properly, difficulties in a pastor's marriage significantly increase the chances of crossing boundaries in ministry.

Loss

Perhaps the deepest crises any of us face—and the source of our keenest personal vulnerability—come from loss. Most often experienced in relation to the death of a close friend or relative, loss can also result from divorce or other profound estrangement from what was once a primary relationship. And then there are the losses suffered from within: the loss of an expected future when a medical diagnosis is grim, or of an anticipated joy when a couple is told they cannot have children. Finally, there are the gradual losses of taken-for-granted abilities that can come with aging or illness, where what one loses is oneself, or at least the self one knows and prizes.

Such losses bring grief—a weight that can settle over a soul, blocking out light and air. It can color memory with such sorrow and longing as to be unbearable, turn the present into a painful slog to be gotten through by any means necessary, and leave the future only an object of dread. Normally grief resolves with time, but for major life losses the time frame for even initial recovery averages two years.[14] In addition, one may suffer what doctors call complications of grief, where the healing process is arrested for whatever reason and one remains stuck or sinks into clinical depression. There are different degrees of loss and different kinds of grieving, and not all of them are experienced as devastating. But whatever the level of grief, it must be faced squarely and worked through, not suppressed or

14. Thérèse Rando, *How to Go on Living when Someone You Love Dies* (New York: Bantam, 1991), 76–77.

evaded. Grief avoided goes underground for a time, but eventually it reemerges. When it returns, it often comes in a toxic and destructive form. Pastors should not deny or sideline their own suffering when losses are profound. Instead, in these times of increased personal and professional risk, they should seek the appropriate forms of support and time for healing.

Professional Setbacks

Of a different order altogether are the professional frustrations and disappointments that can occur over a lifetime in ministry. Depending on the polity and organization of one's church or denomination, the path to desired professional rewards and responsibilities may be through a bishop or district superintendent who appoints pastors to their charges. It may involve a committee or commission that matches candidates to posts, or a process that resembles applying for an executive or academic position, where a search committee selects possible candidates from a pool of applicants to come for visits, interviews, and a trial sermon. None of these processes are foolproof, and they are liable sometimes to go awry, resulting in mismatches between the needs of a congregation and the gifts and vision of its selected leader.

At times highly competent pastors languish in posts that give them little opportunity to use their gifts (though the best of these will often pour themselves into ministry and flourish nonetheless). In other cases, pastors are placed in positions clearly over their heads, demanding abilities or interests they lack and causing both pastor and congregation to suffer as a result. Ministers may sometimes believe that they are the victim of such a mismatch, the result of other people's misjudgments, so that they cannot do their best work. Conversely, in an appointment system, they may be moved from a place where they have made great progress, and feel as if they are being forced to start all over again. Whether or not their judgment of the situation is correct, pastors in such circumstances must guard against the temptation to seek validation or reassurance by shifting the ground of their relationship with parishioners. Even if they are not in the right place, or have in fact been unfairly treated, they still must honor their office and their calling by observing the boundaries that protect it.

OTHERS' VULNERABILITIES

So far we have spoken of conditions that make a minister more susceptible to confusion, self-deception, or moral failure. But the same conditions of increased vulnerability can apply to congregants as well. In fact, people are much more likely to seek pastoral help when they *are* emotionally vulnerable. Therefore, all the risks that go with the fatigue or loneliness, conflict or loss may also arise from those receiving pastoral care. It is entirely possible that a congregant or counselee, seeking comfort or affirmation in the midst of a painful situation, could actively seek to shift the character of the relationship from pastoral to romantic or sexual. When the special dynamics of transference are added to the equation, this risk is only increased. However, none of this changes the moral picture or diminishes the pastor's duty to maintain a space where the congregant is safe, including safe from his or her own destructive impulses. The professional power of the ministry gives ministers the authority, and the responsibility, to keep protective boundaries in place.

Being Alert to Danger Signals

Over many years of working in this field, I have had a number of conversations with people in ministry who have become involved to a greater or lesser degree in inappropriate romantic or sexual relationships. Some of these have been between pastors and congregants, others between pastors and those they supervise in ministry, and still others between professional peers both of whom had covenants to honor elsewhere. I have talked to both clergy and laypeople in these situations, across a variety of circumstances. Most of these were intelligent and successful people, people of broad experience, who had excellent social skills and who, one would think, knew what they were doing. And after the fact, at least, they were able to identify quite clearly what was wrong with the decisions they made and the actions they took.

Nevertheless, I have heard over and over in these conversations one or another variation on "I didn't see it coming." Despite my initial skepticism, I have come to believe that most of them did *not* in fact see the trouble they were heading into until they had long since crossed important psychological lines. By the time they became fully aware of what they were doing, they had already forged new bonds and invested in a new strategy for dealing with whatever issue drove them, making it excruciatingly hard to withdraw. Very few managed to back away from the cliff in time. As a result, many did real harm to others as well as to themselves, fracturing churches and causing suffering to the innocent.

This does not mean that these people had no capacity to act otherwise than they did, or that they were not responsible for their choices. It also doesn't mean that they fell into wrongdoing all at once and without warning. What it means is that people in the grip of need or desire, people in pain or flirting with despair, frequently avert their gazes from the signs that they are in danger because they don't want to know. More precisely, they can't afford to see what is happening because they don't know how to go on without the comfort or the affirmation, the renewed hope or the rekindled interest in living that the inappropriate relationship seems to offer them, and so they choose blindness. In a very real sense, they do *not* see what is coming, even if that lack of foresight is not innocent.

Some writers in this arena have argued that any attention to psychological factors in clergy misconduct amounts to making excuses for offenders.[15] I respectfully disagree. The point here is not to exonerate ministers who violate the trust bestowed on them, which is a grave and often a devastating matter. It is rather to learn what we can about the signs that indicate when such a violation is imminent and to try to penetrate the self-deception that is so critical an element in misconduct. We want to put in place all the barriers we can to prevent actions whose repercussions can destroy families, shatter churches, and take more than a generation to heal.

Below I discuss a number of danger signals, some of which are drawn from existing literature focusing on the signs that indicate when a person is at risk,[16] but many of which come from the insights and

15. For instance, Ann-Janine Morey refers to an article identifying risk factors in pastoral care as blaming women while depicting offending pastors as "misguided but innocent victims of circumstance" ("Blaming Women for the Sexually Abusive Male Pastor," *Christian Century*, October 5, 1988, 867).
16. Richard M. Gula, *Ethics in Pastoral Ministry* (New York: Paulist Press, 1996), 112–16; Marilyn R. Peterson, *At Personal Risk: Boundary Violations in Professional-Client Relationship* (New York: Norton, 1992), 72–102.

experiences of those who either have been guilty of boundary viola-tions in the past or have come perilously close and have been willing to talk with me about it. To be clear, these are not merely signals that caution is warranted; they are indications that the character of a relationship has begun to shift and that the minister is *already in trouble*. The behavior described below represents a continuum from mild indications of sexual interest to frank experiences of physical attraction and intense desire. By the time one reaches the end of the spectrum, what remains is only the overt behavior that expresses the shift that has occurred. One person describing the history of an il-licit relationship put it aptly: "We were lovers already. We just hadn't slept together yet." This is not to say that the presence or absence of sexual contact does not matter; physical intimacy itself creates new bonds and does fresh harm both to the participants and to their spouses if they are married. But stopping just short of sex acts does not constitute fulfilling obligations as a minister. As one pastor said to me in reflecting on the events that led to a past violation, "The line is always a lot farther back than you tell yourself."

GIVING SPECIAL ATTENTION TO APPEARANCE

When a pastor finds that he or she gets dressed up when expecting to see a particular parishioner or colleague—paying more attention to personal grooming or clothing, hair or makeup than usual—this is a sign that the pastor is no longer focused on the care to be provided or the work to be done together. The literal purpose of trying to look "attractive" is to "attract" another. Thus, paying special attention to appearance indicates that the professional encounter has subtly shifted toward courtship or dating—or at least that the pastor is seeking appreciation and affirmation as a gendered and sexual being. This is extremely easy to rationalize, but the behavior signals danger.

BECOMING MENTALLY PREOCCUPIED

It is normal for a dedicated pastor to be concerned about the people in her or his charge, especially if one of them is having an especially difficult time. If a parishioner is dealing with a family crisis or a serious illness, grieving after a major loss or struggling with depression, it is natural that this person should come into the pastor's mind, not to mention his or her prayers, from time to time. It is also natural for the pastor to make an effort to stay in closer touch than usual. But when the pastor begins thinking about an individual constantly or recurrently, wondering all day long where he is or what she is doing, imagining his voice or her face when there is no obvious reason for it, this is a danger signal that normal pastoral concern has become unhealthy preoccupation, and something beyond pastoral interest is at work.

Altering, Extending, or Increasing the Frequency of Meeting Times

The church is an organization that depends heavily on the participation of volunteers, many of whom also have jobs and families. Thus, it is not surprising that it can be a challenge for pastors to find times when people in the church who need to work together can meet. It is not uncommon for pastors to catch a committee chair at lunch or to grab coffee with a lay leader on her way into the office in the morning. And the same flexibility in scheduling appointments beyond the regular workday often applies to meetings for the purpose of offering pastoral care or counsel. For this reason, as we suggested in chapter 3, pastors are encouraged to set aside one evening a week for appointments, scheduled at regular intervals. This practice establishes a routine that helps to reinforce the nature and purpose of such meetings, and keeps them clearly within the rubric of pastoral work. This schedule need not be utterly rigid as some circumstances call for an exception, but if a pastor regularly extends appointments beyond the allotted hour, frequently makes special arrangements, or juggles other obligations in order to be available to a particular congregant, this is another danger signal that other dynamics are in play besides the desire to be of pastoral assistance.

The same observations apply to meeting with a particular congregant more frequently than every week or two, or extending the period of regular meetings beyond the two to six sessions that are the norm in short-term intervention. Failing to refer a congregant to another counselor when the congregant's needs exceed the pastor's office and level of training indicates that something other than the spiritual care of the congregant is driving the minister's behavior, another sign of danger.

Seeking One-on-One Interaction

Much of the work of the church is done by groups of people, and even when only two people are directly involved in a particular matter, the presence of other people is generally not a problem. Most meetings can occur at a table in the fellowship hall during coffee hour. Of course, some conversations involve confidential information or sensitive issues, where it is necessary to protect a measure of privacy. But when the pastor begins to prefer meeting with a particular individual alone even when nothing requires such protection, or feels a twinge of irritation when someone else joins the table where a conversation with that individual is taking place, these feelings require close examination as indications that the character of the relationship has shifted.

Offering Inappropriate Personal Disclosures

In chapter 3, I talked about the delicate balance between appropriate openness and maintaining professional boundaries as it relates to what personal information a minister shares. The most useful criterion for what to share is what serves the pastor's calling as a teacher, example, and guide, helping her or him to be an effective leader and shepherd. Disclosing personal matters to a congregant or counselee when the pastoral office is not served thereby, when it is the minister's needs that are being met rather than the parishioner's, signals a breakdown in the pastor's role in relation to this person. Such a reversal of roles is a regular precursor to other kinds of boundary violations.

Preferring Another's Company

When pastors who are married or in a committed relationship come to prefer the company of someone from their ministry setting to that of their partner, they are in serious trouble. This is the case whether the other individual is a congregant, a counselee, or a colleague in ministry, even if there has been no word or gesture expressing romantic or sexual interest on either side. Emotional bonds that grow out of simple liking or shared work are powerful, and they often develop in a context protected from the interpersonal challenges and practical difficulties that strain our primary partnerships. Ministers cannot reason that they are "just friends" with someone who becomes their preferred companion in enjoyment and relaxation. Failing to recognize the significance of such a transfer of personal intimacy is the beginning of many transgressions about which pastors later say, "I never meant for it to happen." Preference for an individual from the ministry setting signals a need to reestablish a measure of distance in the work relationship, and also to address the state of the relationship with one's partner, perhaps with the aid of a counselor.

Changing the Kind or Frequency of Touch

In movies, people who have been strenuously refusing to admit sexual interest in someone suddenly drop all pretenses and sweep the other into their arms. In real life, the move toward an overt physical expression of desire is much more likely to come in stages. A reassuring touch on the hand becomes more prolonged until the two are holding hands; a quick supportive hug is extended until it is a full embrace; with a sudden turn of the head, an affectionate peck on the cheek becomes a real kiss. Of course, some degree of physical touch is an ordinary element in caring for people in crisis. It is a powerful tool for offering compassion, reassurance, and support to someone in trouble—part of the work a pastor is called to do. Therefore, the line between appropriate and unethical conduct toward congregants cannot be drawn simply by saying, "Keep your hands to yourself." Instead, deciding when, whether, and how to touch someone in one's care must be a matter of sensitivity to the other's needs and of keen awareness of one's own motives and vulnerabilities. For this reason, changes in the kind or frequency of touch should set off alarm bells; they are significant indications of changing dynamics in a relationship. They provide pastors an occasion to reexamine their own emotional state and often signal a need to reestablish necessary distance, perhaps by referring care to another pastor.

Shielding Contact from View

Many of the preceding signs are at least somewhat open to interpretation. It is not *impossible* to offer an innocuous explanation for them, even if such an explanation is not the likeliest one (which is why rationalization in these matters is so easy). But once a pastor confronts the fact that he or she is taking measures to keep the frequency, duration, or circumstances of the time spent with anyone in the ministry setting from being known to other people, the realm of ambiguity has been left behind. Whether the pastor acknowledges this or not, steps have been taken that will make sexual intimacy a practical possibility. Meanwhile, the pastor has created a secret and is pulling the congregant or colleague into it. At this point, the pastor is already in violation of her or his professional responsibilities to care for and protect this person, and is thus far down the road toward actionable misconduct.

Deceiving One's Partner or Spiritual Guide

The most telling form of shielding behavior from sight is deceiving one's partner or spiritual director (in the case, for example, of one who has taken a vow of celibacy) about it. It matters very little whether this deception takes the form of lying outright or simply of keeping silent about the shape of this relationship or the importance it is coming to have. Saying nothing about a significant relationship clearly indicates knowledge that the relationship is problematic, even if one pretends otherwise. The experience of lying to or deliberately hiding the truth from an intimate partner or confidant may bring one up short, forcing a confrontation with how far things have gone. If it does, this may be the last opportunity to avert further harm. The pastor must immediately tell someone the truth about what is going on and get help in stopping it before it goes any further. While it is very hard to do this, it is not nearly as hard as the likely road that lies ahead for the one who does nothing.

Indulging in Sexual Fantasy

When one begins indulging in sexual fantasy about another person, this indicates that the relationship has already been fully sexualized, even if no physical sexual contact has occurred. While actual sex acts have a distinctive significance of their own, sexuality is as much a matter of ideas, feelings, and longings as it is of genital behavior. We enact with our bodies desires and intentions that reside first in mind, heart, and imagination. It is the connection between the inner self and outward behavior that gives sex its unitive power and its capacity to be a potent force in human life, whether for good or ill.

In contemporary society, there is a fair amount of foolishness and patent dishonesty about all this, to the extreme of public figures swearing that they had not had "sexual relations" with a person simply because vaginal intercourse had not occurred. Along with using an unreasonably narrow definition of what sex is, we frequently speak as if only the body "counts" in sexual life. Thus, even some literature in the ethics of ministry treats indulging in sexual fantasy about a congregant or colleague as morally insignificant, regarding it as simply unreal and therefore unimportant.[17] This betrays a remarkably narrow understanding. A pastor who deliberately entertains sexual fantasies about a member of the community has already made that person a means to his or her own sexual gratification. It is no longer possible to pretend that this is someone the pastor is simply there to care for as a shepherd, or is primarily a person with whom the pastor shares the work of serving a community. Moreover, the odds of continuing this practice over any period of time without ever reaching out to make the fantasy actual are extremely low. As ethicist Margaret Farley wisely counsels, "You must not begin to go in imagination where you do not wish to end up in reality."[18]

Becoming Physically Aroused

Along with pretending that only bodily acts have any bearing on our moral and spiritual lives, we can also convince ourselves that even active sexual desire is merely an inward psychological state, not a problem unless one acts to satisfy it. (This is the sort of rationalizing people can only believe because they want to so badly.) In truth, a person in a state of sexual arousal not only feels different on the inside; she or he also looks different to others. Among the subtler signs of arousal are dilation of the pupils, flushing, elevated body temperature, rapid breathing, and perspiration. Even assuming nothing overt is said or done, all these signs of sexual excitement are detectable, and they may provoke a strong response from the other party, anything from excitement to fear, dismay, or profound shock. Becoming physically

17. Richard Gula, *Just Ministry: Professional Ethics for Pastoral Ministers* (New York: Paulist Press, 2007), 166–68.

18. Margaret Farley, *Personal Commitments: Beginning, Keeping, Changing* (New York: HarperCollins, 1990), 127.

aroused in response to a congregant or ministerial colleague can have disastrous consequences for one's personal and professional life and, more important, can do harm to the person one is supposed to be serving. In addition, when in a state of intense arousal, one perceives, judges, and thinks differently. In the grip of desire, we tend to see and remember the things that accord with what we want rather than the broader picture. Moreover, the biochemistry of arousal works to reduce inhibitions, making it harder to control impulses, so that one is more likely to act on desire. The pastor who tries to work as a professional colleague or pastor with someone to whom he or she has such an intense physical response is playing Russian roulette.

Responding When You Realize You're in Trouble

WHEN ON THE EDGE

Suppose you are a pastor who has come to see that you are at serious risk in some relationship in your ministry—with a colleague, someone you supervise, a parishioner, or a counselee. You have not yet done anything that constitutes overt professional misconduct, but you recognize that the character of this relationship has shifted so that it now serves as a context for your own needs for appreciation or emotional intimacy to be met, a place for you to feel needed, admired, or loved. Your role as a shepherd has been compromised, and you are already in trouble. This is a painful recognition, and difficult to accept, not least because it means that the relationship on which you have come to rely must change dramatically or end altogether. It takes a degree of courage even to come this far, but you also need to act, and quickly, in order to avoid rationalizing your way right back onto the road to disaster. Below are four steps you must take at this stage and one to consider.

> *(1) Tell someone.* The first step is to disclose your situation to someone you can trust to support you but also to hold you firmly accountable. Depending on the circumstances and your life situation, this might be an old friend in whose spiritual wisdom and seriousness you have reason for confidence. It might be a colleague in ministry outside your immediate setting, someone with sufficient strength and independence of judgment to confront you and call you back if you are wandering into danger again.

An established spiritual director or accountability partner is an obvious candidate for this role, provided that you are prepared to abandon whatever pretense has kept this issue from being addressed sooner. If you are married, your spouse may be best able to help you establish the boundaries you need and to keep them in place, as she or he has the largest stake in the resolution. But this will be an alarming and painful process for your partner as well, and it requires a degree of health and stability in the relationship that may not be present. If your marriage is already in a state of conflict or alienation, it may be wiser to begin with another counselor who can help you address both the inappropriate professional relationship and the issues within your marriage. Whomever you choose to go to for help, you must tell that person the whole truth. Do not justify, minimize, edit, or focus on what hasn't happened yet. Tell your confidant everything you know and suspect about what is going on inside you as well as outside, everything that persuades you that you are in real trouble. Be unsparing. It is no kindness to yourself to avoid facing the worst, as it is likely to come back to haunt you if you don't face it now.

(2) *Back up*. You must act immediately to place distance between yourself and the person in relation to whom you are in trouble. If this person is a counselee, refer him or her to someone else for ongoing care right away. If it is a parishioner with whom you have worked closely on church projects, turn over responsibility for overseeing this area to another minister or lay leader if at all possible. If not, alter the constellation of responsibilities and the pattern of collaboration so that your work is no longer one-on-one and you never meet alone. If it is a partner in ministry, a colleague or someone you supervise, do everything in your power to change the structure of your interaction, reducing the amount of time you spend together and shifting it to group contexts. When you must meet, do so in public and in formal settings. In all these instances, avoid anything that looks or feels like a social occasion or like a personal encounter between friends. You are working to restore the character of a pastoral relationship that has gone awry; what feels normal or natural to you is

now a terrible guide. Far better to feel uncomfortably formal and awkward than to try to smooth everything over, which is likely to lead you back into familiar but dangerous territory. If the other person feels the change and finds it strange, this may be uncomfortable, but it is a good sign.

(3) *Resist the temptation to talk to the individual involved about your feelings or the issues you are having.* No matter how good your intentions, a conversation about how you are attracted or inappropriately attached serves only to further sexualize the relationship. If the person has not been aware of your feelings, such a conversation will make her or him aware, and saying some version of "I cannot continue to be this close to you" is the equivalent of telling someone, "Don't think about pelicans." It can hardly help bringing about the very thing it disavows. If the person has been aware of your attraction, she or he will understand your changed behavior as much as is needed. In either case, this is not his or her problem to deal with but yours.

(4) *Uncover and address the underlying issues.* It is vitally important that you understand the circumstances that made you vulnerable to boundary crossing—whether a matter of loneliness or professional frustration, spiritual malaise or conflict at home—and the needs that you were channeling into this inappropriate relationship. If you do not do this basic work, you may forestall one illicit relationship only to find your way into another when unmet needs and unacknowledged problems rear their heads again. Most people will need help with this work, either a professional therapist or a spiritual director or pastoral counselor of special training and long experience.

(5) *Leave.* In cases where the emotional attachment is strong or the degree of romantic or sexual bonding is high, saving your ministry may require leaving the setting. This may seem like a drastic solution, and indeed it is. It may require uprooting your family, sidelining your career in ministry for a time, and disrupting the life of the community you serve. It is a course of last resort that makes sense only when compared to some

of the alternatives that may follow if you choose to stay and do not manage to restore a fully stable professional relationship in place of the distorted one you have developed. Bear in mind that such a restoration may well have to endure for years, through challenges at work and at home when it may be very tempting to seek consolation or personal affirmation by returning to the improper relationship. In addition, the other person also remains an actor in her or his own right. If she or he is facing difficulties, it is quite possible that the congregant or colleague may seek to reestablish the old pattern. Whether you can continue to serve in a professional capacity in proximity to this person with any degree of safety for either of you is a genuine question, and the answer may very well be no.

WHEN OVER THE LINE

Everything thus far in this chapter has been aimed at providing resources and tools to keep pastors from stepping over the line into wrongdoing. But let's now suppose that you are a pastor for whom this counsel has come too late to prevent sexual misconduct. What do you do if you have already crossed the line and are actively involved in a sexual relationship with a colleague, someone you supervise, a congregant, or a counselee?[19] The first and most vital thing is what *not* to do: do not give up on yourself and use your despair as an excuse to continue in a pattern of behavior that is not only flatly immoral but also a betrayal of your calling and your community. Throwing up your hands at this point (whether hoping to avoid detection indefinitely or just waiting for someone else to intervene from outside) is a form of self-indulgence that only adds cowardice to other offenses. It expresses a willingness to see more harm come to other people rather than resolving to face painful consequences, which will in all likelihood come nonetheless. And even if you are among the small minority who manage never to get caught, the price you will pay

---

19. In all of what follows, I am assuming that all parties are of the age of consent, and that no threats or other forms of coercion are involved—in short, that no actual crime has been committed. If this is not the case, and extortion, forcible or statutory rape, or sexual abuse of a minor are in question, you have no alternative but to involve the police.

in forfeited self-respect and the damage to your inmost self as you become a practiced deceiver and an abuser of trust are incalculable. The only alternative to despair is faith, confidence in the gospel you were commissioned to preach. The conviction that there is no place to which we can bring ourselves that is too far for God's mercy to reach is the only thing that can give you the strength to face where you have come and to turn away. Remember that the grace of God is more than pardon; it is God's faithfulness to walk beside us and God's power to transform. The following are the practical steps to be taken as you look for the way forward. They are based on my conversations with violators, church officials, and supervisors as well as on social scientific research on patterns and results of clergy misconduct.[20]

(1) *Stop.* There is no middle ground here. Do not hope somehow to make things better while continuing the behavior or to find some gradual way to bring things to a tidy close. Such vain hopes are just a sign of continued self-deception. Whatever the concrete shape of the unethical relationship, it must end, altogether and right now. This is the first step.

(2) *Find a trustworthy counselor to walk through this process with you.* For this you need a person of wisdom and integrity, someone who will hold your confidence but who will not lie to you or for you, and who will in no way let you off the hook.[21] It must also be someone who can and will take the time needed to pray with you, listen to you, give you counsel, and offer you steady accompaniment through the long work of repentance, for this is no momentary matter. It will include not just the immediate change of behavior but making what amends are possible and beginning the long-term work of recovery and healing.

(3) *Part responsibly from the victim of your misconduct.* This step is both dangerous and necessary if you are not to add one more

---

20. See in particular Garland and Arguenta, "How Clergy Sexual Misconduct Happens," 1–27.

21. Bear in mind that in many denominational structures, other clergy or church officials may be under an obligation to report sexual misconduct when they become aware of it.

layer to your mistreatment of this person by seeming to abandon her or him, as if you were the injured party. No matter how this behavior began, no matter who initiated what, *you are responsible*, and you must own that responsibility forthrightly in a face-to-face conversation. To minimize the chance that this painful confrontation will simply provide another occasion to seek your own comfort in this person, meet in a visible space with other people around. Allot a brief time for the conversation, and arrange a timely follow-up call with your counselor. In the conversation with the victim, make it clear that you are fully and finally withdrawing from this improper relationship. Apologize for the harm you have done and the suffering you have caused (whether or not the other person recognizes it as such). Explain the options the other person now has, including how to go about reporting you to the appropriate church authorities for misconduct. You should also provide referrals for pastoral care or therapeutic help for this person and do everything in your power to be sure that this help is genuinely available to him or her, including offering funds to pay for it if needed.

It will be evident that all these actions present real risks to your personal and professional future; a person who feels rejected may decide to file a report of abuse, which is not unjustified. There simply is no course of action that forecloses the possibility that your career and your reputation will be destroyed, along with your family if you are married. (To state what should be obvious, continuing the behavior will only increase the likelihood of such an outcome.) These were the risks to which you opened yourself when you chose this path.

(4) Seek long-term skilled care and spiritual direction for yourself to understand and address the personal issues and weaknesses that contributed to your behavior. If you omit this step and attempt to continue to serve as a pastor, you are likely to repeat the misconduct in another setting. If you are not willing to pursue this work, you should leave the ministry. Also, recognize that one possible outcome of such in-depth work might be to conclude that your personal vulnerabilities are such that you cannot safely continue in pastoral ministry.

(5) Be as transparent as possible. If the other party decides not to file
a report, you must decide in consultation with your counselor
whether to report your own actions to the appropriate super-
visory authorities of your church. Doing so has the benefits of
transparency and accountability to the community that called
and commissioned you. But beware of using full disclosure hastily as a strategy for assuaging your guilt without regard for its
impact on others' lives. In your decision, you must consider the
consequences of submitting to the process of your denomination
for all the people affected. Many church protocols for dealing
with pastoral misconduct require formal hearings and deposi-
tions. This makes it essentially certain that family members
of both parties as well as the entire congregation and many
outside of it will come to know at least the broad outline of
events. The repercussions in fractured churches, broken marriages, and disillusioned believers can be devastating. Again,
these consequences are part of what you signed on for when
you made the choices you did. However, many others who had
no such choices are liable to suffer for them as well.

(6) Adopt and follow your community's disciplines. If you decide
not to self-report, recognize that you are entering very dangerous territory with many opportunities for self-deception. You
must at a minimum impose on yourself the requirements your
denomination would impose on you if you had, and do so under
the guidance and oversight of a trusted counselor. These may
include an extended period of time away from active ministry,
long-term therapy, close supervision in future ministry, or other
sanctions. These are intended both to help you in the work
of recovery and restitution and to protect the church against
the possibility of future misconduct. Voluntarily submitting
yourself to the conditions of reinstatement your community
would require is a minimal indication of good faith, and a way
of stepping back toward the covenant you have broken.

5

Embracing the Practices
That Sustain Faithfulness

In the preceding chapters, I have given an account of the character of ministry as a distinctive profession in order to place its ethical obligations within a broader framework. I have also discussed the peculiar risks and challenges of pastoral service and the resources needed to meet them. My aim has been to offer practical guidelines and tools to help a person remain, and indeed flourish, within the moral constraints of ministry. But as I've repeatedly emphasized, fulfilling the ethical requirements of ministry goes beyond having the right ideas and information, and requires far more than the ability to articulate and justify a set of rules of conduct. Developing the resources to be a good shepherd to a Christian community is the work of a whole life. It is a matter of being and becoming the right person as much as of knowing and doing the right things. In keeping with the emphasis on an ethic of virtue as central to Christian moral understanding, I now turn from the work of instruction in pastoral ethics to the more fundamental work of moral and spiritual formation that undergirds the possibility of faithful service. Without this, no teaching will provide real protection or bear lasting fruit.

In an important sense, then, I am ending where I could have
begun. Unless one adopts and clings to the spiritual practices laid
out in this chapter in some form, it is hard to see how any of what
went before can be of very much use in the long run. No amount
of understanding of pastoral duties, and no degree of insight into
how and why they can be so difficult to fulfill, will provide the power
to fulfill them in fact over the course of decades in ministry. I can
describe signs of imminent moral failure for pages on end, but that
in itself will not enable pastors to recognize and heed them in time
to save themselves and others: not when they are beset by blindness
and confusion, or overtaken by emptiness and the loss of meaning.
For that they must be illuminated and sustained, nourished and
strengthened, upheld and rescued by a power beyond themselves,
secured and kept safe by God the Holy Spirit. This is the only true
foundation not just of ministry, but indeed of any form of genuinely
Christian existence.

So why save this essential matter for the end of the book? It is
because years of experience in theological education as well as many
conversations with pastors have persuaded me that beginning here
has very little chance of shaping anyone's behavior. It is not that
pastors do not believe that they should practice their faith rather
than just talking about it; it is just that those practices always seem
to us less urgent than the task at hand, whatever that task might be.
The irony of a minister of the gospel feeling that she or he is too
busy to live a Christian life is not lost on us. Still we defer and defer,
shortcut and short-circuit our own spiritual lives until we are preaching and teaching from memory, drawing on some past time when we
had a vital relationship with the living God. If we are not careful,
and if nothing occurs to awaken us from our slumber, we may find
that we have at length fallen into a state that is psychologically hard
to distinguish from unbelief. Such an attenuated form of Christian
faith is not nearly enough to safeguard pastors and the people for
whom they care.

A present threat will often awaken a dormant faith, inspiring at
least the most basic prayer, "Help!" The preceding pages have described the perils that beset the practice of ministry. In them, I have
tried to show how it is possible for pastors to wander only half aware
into a place they would have sworn they would never go, and I have

given a glimpse of the devastation to their lives and communities that could result if they do. I hope all this will startle pastors to wakefulness and cause them to recognize their need for the spiritual practices described in this chapter. Pastors take vows in which they promise faithfulness, which is not an idea but an activity. For the sake of their churches, families, and souls, they must not presume to lead and guide others in a faith they have ceased to inhabit, or try to serve out of a human strength they have ceased to buttress with the grace of God. No one is strong and good enough to make such efforts anything but an expression of foolish arrogance. The disciplines of Christian life are the only thing that can sustain the faith and fidelity essential to ministry. In this chapter I focus on two practices that are especially vital for the life of ministers of the gospel: prayer and accountability.

Prayer

Let me put this as baldly as possible: without prayer, one has no spiritual life. Prayer is more than duty, more than ritual, more than simply one among many practices of Christian faith to be laid alongside getting to church on Sunday or giving up something for Lent. It is also more than the "chatting with God" we sometimes trivialize it as. It is the very lifeblood of Christian existence and the one thing that no outward circumstance can deprive us of. It can sustain us when every other aspect of religious life is stripped away, whether by crippling illness, isolation, the darkness of depression, or the sufferings of persecution. As God breathes life into clay at creation and makes a living soul, so the living breath of the Spirit to which we open ourselves in prayer is the difference between a living member of the body of Christ and a lifelike corpse.

To abandon the life of prayer is not only to fall silent before God, mute in adoration and gratitude as well as in petition; it is in effect to stop one's ears, to close off awareness and attention to the continual presence of God within the soul. This is to undertake to live a religious life on one's own, guided by one's own judgment and supported by one's own goodness. This flies in the face of the most basic convictions of our faith: that God alone is good, wise, holy, and that every human is in need of the healing and restoring work of God made manifest in Jesus Christ and continued in us by the Spirit. A professed Christian who tries to do without the practice of prayer is living out a heresy, no matter how orthodox his or her creed.

For anyone formed by Scripture, this is not a new or surprising idea. The New Testament is full of teaching regarding the necessity of prayer. We see it in every possible form, from the example of Jesus, who regularly sought time alone to pray (Matt. 14:23; Mark 1:35; Luke 6:12; 22:41–44), to the model prayer Jesus gave his disciples (Matt. 6:5–15; Luke 11:1–13), to the admonitions of Paul to pray "continually" (1 Thess. 5:17; cf. Rom. 12:2; Phil. 4:6; Col. 4:2), to the narrative of the first-century church in Acts (e.g., 2:42; 3:1; 6:4–6; 12:12; 13:3; 14:23). Such citations could be multiplied. Everywhere we turn, we find the earliest believers praying, seeking guidance as they appoint leaders or consolation as they wait in prison, and in all circumstances looking for wisdom to know the will of God and for strength to do it. Prayer is the concrete and tangible way to abide in Jesus, which in his parting discourse he tells his followers is the only way to have his life in themselves (John 15:4–6).

Prayer is how we enter into communion with God and how we discern the meaning of Scripture for our lives. It is the space in which we present ourselves to be filled with God's goodness and equipped for God's purposes. It is what enables us to abide in Jesus's word, for it is the time in which the word—both the word of the text and the word of God's own inward witness—comes to abide in us. Apart from prayer it is difficult to imagine how one might be led by God's Spirit and so be among those Paul calls the children of God (Rom. 8:14). Without the steady practice of prayer—not only the formal liturgical prayer shared in the worshiping community but also personal prayer as individuals or in small groups—one risks falling into formalism and emptiness, a state as perilous as any overt crisis of faith because one is unlikely to notice being in it.

All this is true for anyone who aims to live as a Christian in any setting. But it has a special relevance and urgency for people called to lead a Christian community, those who dare to stand in the role of shepherd to the people of God. We have reviewed at length the many risks and challenges of pastoral ministry: the inequalities of knowledge and the aura of divine authority, the dangerous forms of personal power ministers must wield, the necessity of navigating between a chilly remoteness and a false model of friendship, the demands of constant scrutiny, the burdens of frustration and loneliness, and the constant danger of self-deception. While nothing can guarantee surmounting these risks, a serious practice of prayer is the best way to keep them from becoming overwhelming.

The prayer of which I speak here is different in character from the prayers that are official functions of the pastoral office, those pastors are continually called on to read in worship or lead at church events or offer at the hospital bedside. In all of these the pastor speaks for a whole community, indeed for a whole tradition, and not simply in her or his own voice, which is just as it should be. But there must also be a space for the pastor as a needy human being dwelling consciously in God's presence, in speech or in the silent openness that can come when words fall away. Without such a deeply personal practice, it is hard to imagine how anyone could remain long in ministry without risking emotional collapse or moral failure. Those ministers-in-training who have never had such a prayer life, living their whole lives as Christians deprived of this sustenance, can no longer afford to be without it as they enter into ministry.

I have spoken so far only of the risks of trying to serve as a pastor without the support and illumination of prayer. But while some may undertake a spiritual practice out of fear of the alternatives, fear will not keep them in such a practice over time. Instead, my hope is that readers will begin on this path and find in it such nourishment, comfort, and life that they come to cherish and depend on it, and so find it impossible to forgo. In that hope, then, let me say what I can about the gifts that await those whose lives are sustained by disciplined prayer. Note that in what follows, I am speaking of the fruit of a practice of prayer developed over years. God dwells in eternity and thus is ever present and open to us, nearer always than our next breath. We, however, are creatures of time and space. As such, we have no constancy but are always at some point in a cycle of closeness and distance, of acuity and deafness in relation to God. Thus we must learn both to speak and to listen, and learn to wait through the silence and darkness that is sometimes our experience when fears and grief are heavy and what we feel is God's absence.

Gifts of Prayer

RESPITE

Prayer offers us a moment out of time. While somewhere the clock is ticking, entering into the presence of the One who inhabits eternity means laying aside the rushing current of our days with their tasks and demands. We come to be still, to be whole, to be present and alive in this moment that contains all moments, before the Lord whose I AM encompasses all past, present, and future. It is like learning to breathe again.

WELCOME

There is no time when the door is not open, no place too far to return from, no state of bewilderment or doubt or spiritual dishevelment in which one is deemed unfit to appear. Make no mistake: in prayer, all is seen for what it is. Here there can be no subterfuge, no dissembling, no cleaning up an act. And yet the lamp is lit, and the light pours out, and whether dutiful children or late-returning prodigals, we find the Father is in the road to welcome us.

INTIMACY

To one who has never experienced prayer's intimacy, it is impossible to describe the ease of being utterly known, so that evasion is futile and altogether unnecessary. In prayer, like nowhere else on earth, we are free to pour out our hearts, every terror and grief, every half-acknowledged desire or secretly harbored darkness of malice or envy. Any truth can be recognized and named because all is already grasped, laid open to its depths by the unflinching and compassionate gaze of the One who meets our deepest darkness head on and dissolves it in light.

INSIGHT

In the perfect safety of prayer, we are able to see what is otherwise obscured by need or anxiety, by anger or defensiveness. Sheltered a moment from the storm of emotions—our own and other people's—we may find insight into what otherwise is maddening or simply perplexing in us or in others. Such insight certainly does not end the difficulties, but it is often the beginning of their resolution.

SELF-KNOWLEDGE

In earnest prayer, we find that the Lord—who has searched and known us (Ps. 139:1)—discloses to us as much truth about ourselves as we are able to bear. This is not always a happy experience, but it remains a blessing and an honor nonetheless, for it is a mark of our existence as spiritual beings who are called into free and loving union with a holy God. The one prerequisite of grace is to know our need of it. To those in ministry, such self-knowledge is an indispensable gift.

WARNING

One aspect of the self-knowledge bestowed in prayer is the gift of seeing when and how we are in spiritual peril—a crucial gift because our capacity to avert our gaze from what we do not wish to see is nearly limitless. Coming to hear, much less to heed, such warnings is not the work of a moment, however. To have our ears unstopped requires that we have our hearts converted, for we must first become willing to know the truth. But we do not wait for our wills to change so that we may pray sincerely. We wait *in* prayer, in the presence of the One whose healing we seek, praying to desire what we need so that we may receive it.

CONVICTION

Often the truth we most need to hear is of the remaining power of evil in our lives: how much we remain captive to false fears and desires, how deeply we have grieved the love of God by our devotion to other deities or our indifference to other people. Even in such conviction there is blessing, for to have our own sin revealed to us is also to be recalled from a far country toward the home we have deserted. As poet Constance Black has written, "Contrition's sadness is sweet, because within it is the certainty that Love is at work."[1]

STRENGTH

Neither warning nor conviction is of any use to us unless we find the strength needed to turn back from the road we are on. Yet the whole

---

1. Constance Black, "Repentance," in *Litany of Days & Other Poems* (Provincetown, MA: Fire & Light, 1997).

potency of sin is that it is more than something we do and more than a problem that we have; it is at the same time a condition we are in and a reality that somehow claims us. But this is no barrier to prayer. We can come to prayer empty-handed, confessing that "there is no health in us"[2] and asking for the strength we lack to change course. And when the path that lies before us is straight but seems long, wearisome, and beyond what we can bear, when what fails us is just the strength to go on, here too there is no shame in admitting, "I cannot—unless you help."

CONSOLATION

Life is laced through with sorrows. Some of these simply befall us, conditions of being alive in mortal bodies and loving those we can lose. Others we inflict on ourselves: painful regrets for things we have done or left undone, the bitter fruit of self-will or foolishness or neglect. And some of the pains we suffer are the result of others' actions, intentional or not. Whatever losses we ache with, whatever sad discoveries of betrayal—our own as well as other people's—darken our hearts, prayer offers the place to lay it all open without pretense or reservation. We need not say it right, or even find words at all. We can come as we find ourselves, stunned to silence or wracked with weeping. Jesus knows all about tears, and he can console us.

PEACE

The peace that comes to us in prayer is a mystery; it is not possible to explain but only to experience. God can grant serenity and even joy in the midst of the deepest struggle and grief. Jesus's promise of peace was given to the disciples on the very brink of his crucifixion (John 14:27), and his admonition not to let their hearts be troubled or afraid must have seemed even stranger in retrospect. Surely it did not cancel out their anguish or perplexity. But Jesus kept his promise not to leave them desolate, as he keeps it to this day to us who believe on account of their testimony (John 17:20). In prayer we find that we are never abandoned, and we may find in God's company a sweetness and a solace that can sustain us even when everything else on which we have relied is forfeited.

2. Prayer of Confession, Order for Morning Prayer, Book of Common Prayer.

Models of Prayer

Countless patterns and practices of prayer are to be found along the sweep of Christian history and across the breadth of Christian communities around the globe. Some of these are highly formal and structured, while others are completely free-form and spontaneous. Some prayer disciplines, such as *lectio divina*, use meditation on a biblical text, such as a psalm, or on a single word or image from the text. Some involve a particular posture or a pattern of physical gestures and movements, a pattern often found in penitential prayer in Catholic and Orthodox communities. Other practices are centered by musical repetition (e.g., the meditative prayer songs of the Taizé community) or by the repetition of a central, basic petition (e.g., the Jesus Prayer: "Lord Jesus Christ, Son of God, have mercy on me, a sinner"). Still other forms of prayer are entirely silent, and some follow sustained periods of silence with vocal prayer. Some forms of prayer use a bodily activity of some kind to draw one more deeply into the space of quiet openness before God—anything from walking a maze to controlled breathing to handling beads or stones that serve as markers for themes in meditation (e.g., praying the rosary).

These variations in form are not of special importance in themselves, except insofar as a person or group has developed a familiar pattern that serves to usher them more readily into focused attentiveness and receptivity. Those shaped in a particular practice they find sustaining should by all means continue in it. For those who are beginning what they aim to have become a regular and nourishing prayer discipline, it generally does not matter what form they adopt, so long as it is one they are able to follow steadily over time. (Though there are practical matters to consider—walking prayer may not serve well someone living in a cramped apartment in a Minnesota January who does not tolerate the cold!) To a significant extent what opens our heart and life before God depends simply on what we are accustomed to and how our experience has shaped our thinking and habits concerning prayer.

While the form of prayer adopted is not of great significance, three elements are essential. First, the practice must be *regular* in the sense of being frequent and consistent enough to provide ongoing support and renewal. Having a regular practice of prayer need not mean that one must pray at the same time every day or use the same form every time, nor even that prayer must necessarily be a daily discipline. Although many people find prayer at the beginning or end of every day a helpful checkpoint, it might be that attending (not leading!) a weekly prayer service, meeting once a week with a prayer partner, and observing one extended time of individual silent prayer per week on a day when not rushed will serve one very well. What matters is being brought back to awareness and attention, to reflectivity and receptivity, at short enough intervals that there is not time to wander too far into confusion or forgetfulness. It is the regularity of the practice that enables one to find sustenance in God rather than in some other relationship or activity.

Second, prayer must be *extended* enough in time to allow for working through the welter of worries, distractions, and preoccupations that each of us carries into prayer. Perhaps the single most common barrier to a genuine prayer life in our world is the pace of our lives, their inward pace as much as their rushed and overscheduled outward aspects. We are busy at every moment, minds crowded with anxieties and to-do lists even when we try to settle down to sleep. Or we're stuck in traffic, fingers tapping the steering wheel in impatience. Despite the popularity of instant answers ("Three Minutes to Enlightenment!"), the truth is that spiritual life takes time—time to lay aside the press of tasks enough to attend to the presence and goodness of God here and now, and time to still the inner chatter sufficiently to hear the voice of the Spirit saying "welcome" and "peace." For this reason, whatever form of prayer we undertake, we must keep a protected space for it and not try to cram it into the twelve-minute interval while we are waiting for the next meeting to start. Practically, what this means is to set aside a reasonably extended time safe from interruption, a minimum of thirty minutes for individual silent prayer or an hour if it begins by hearing prayer requests from partners before turning to prayer. In my own experience, as persons become more formed in this practice, two things happen: first, they more readily enter into the inner quiet that makes both hearing and truthful speech possible, and, second, they find the time to pass more quickly so that they come to its close wishing for more. Indeed, there may be seasons of trouble or perplexity or deep challenge when people need more frequent and extended time in prayer in order to be upheld.

Third, prayer must be *honest*. It is astonishing how often we stand in the presence of the Omniscient and recite words that do not pass the most basic test of plausibility. There is no risk of deceiving God, but there is considerable risk of deceiving ourselves and thus going away with our real needs unrecognized, unnamed, and unmet. The idea that prayer must be fully honest in order to offer spiritual sustenance would seem to go without saying. Yet we are quite in the habit of praying (as we are of singing) words that we would have difficulty saying with a straight face. We recite humble prayers of confession while actually feeling pretty good about our performance, and we praise God's abundant blessings while still harboring envy and resentment about what we do not have. We pray that God's will be done when a moment's reflection would make it clear that we are not at all sure we want it, and we ask that we be forgiven without even considering the forgiveness we might be called on to offer those who have wronged us. Our prayers of self-dedication and devotion to the purposes of God are all hedged about with unspoken reservations, places we will not go and assignments we will not undertake.

The point here is not that we must come to prayer in a state of sanctity, full of humility and ready to embrace our enemies. Nor is it that we must already have reached the serene resignation of the saints who can consign themselves joyfully and without reserve to the will of God. The point is merely that it is better not to lie in prayer about the state we're in. Some of the prayers we say in church are in fact the prayers of the saints, or come to us directly from Scripture, even from the mouth of Jesus himself when the disciples asked him, "Teach us to pray" (Luke 11:1). These we should not lay aside, certainly, but it is important that we remain honest enough with ourselves to feel the distance between the words we say and the present state of our hearts. Often we can only pray such prayers as expressions of aspiration, ways of yearning toward the perfect love that casts out fear so that we might say with an undivided heart, "Your will be done" (Matt. 6:10). In the meantime, we must remember the difference between aspiration and reality. This is the only way we can receive the Spirit's illumination and know the truth about the state we are in—and the only way we can ask for the help we truly need.

I recognize that this advice is easier to give than to follow, for it has been my experience that regular, extended, and honest prayer is something one must learn to do. Each person must find an approach that works for her or him in order for it to become a nurturing and sustaining practice, and for me at least this has taken time and effort. For five or six years, my most regular form of Sunday worship was attending a silent Meeting for Worship[3] with a local congregation of the Religious Society of Friends (Quakers). I had been a practicing Christian for forty years at the time and had followed (with greater or less constancy) a number of models and disciplines of individual and small-group prayer over those years. Still, I initially found an hour of sitting in silence and attempting to pray very difficult. I struggled with distractions and preoccupations both inward and outward, and would often be in a state of suppressed irritation rather than worshipfulness by the time the hour closed. Since this was my husband's preferred community of worship, I worked hard to find a way to participate that would be beneficial (or at least not harmful). Below I outline an approach that I eventually developed, which came to be a source of profound nourishment and peace. There is nothing special about this approach; it just happens to be what worked for me. Over the years since I developed it, I have introduced it to groups of students or church members in workshops on spiritual disciplines, and many have found it helpful. I offer it here as one model that might be of use to those looking to deepen their practice of prayer.

An Invitation to Sustained Silent Prayer

To begin, seat yourself comfortably in a place in which you can reasonably count on not being interrupted. You may find it most helpful to close your eyes or to light a candle as a visual focus point, its flame a reminder of the active, dynamic presence of the Spirit of God in the silence.

As you settle down to pray, first let yourself be aware of all the sensory input that enters your consciousness: what you see (the room, the flickering candle), hear (the background noises of the building, the passing traffic, the morning sounds of birds outside), smell (the coffee from breakfast, the tinge of smoke from the candle, the scent of heating wax), feel (the pressure of the seat, the rub of clothing, the

3. The proper name for Quaker worship services.

warmth or coolness of the space), or taste (perhaps sipping a cup of tea during a longer session of prayer). Do not try to suppress these awarenesses as distractions; just note them and respond to them as seems appropriate. You may say a prayer of gratitude for the heating system that keeps your house warm in the winter, for the refrigerator that kicks on and keeps your food safe to eat, for the orderly flow of traffic outside your house, or for the springtime racket of birds in your backyard. Or you might pray for patience for the things that irritate or are unpleasant, for physical discomforts or annoyances that surround you. Naming and praying about these things allows them to recede from the center of consciousness.

After you have dealt with the things your body brings to your awareness, deal with the things your ever-turning mind brings there: chores to do, frustrations to cope with, anxieties to manage, ideas or problems to process, people and situations you are worried about or troubled by. Do not try to avoid these thoughts or to put them out of your mind. Instead, name them directly and let yourself feel fully all the emotions they raise in you. All of these situations and the feelings they cause are safe to bring before God. Then ask and listen to hear what (if anything) you can and should do about those things, and resolve to do it. Write a letter, finish a task, make a call, stay in intentional prayer for someone, bring a meal, offer an apology, visit and listen, send money, carry a gift, offer practical help with a problem—whatever it is, listen and be ready to say yes to those promptings. (When feeling beleaguered you may find it helpful to jot down reminders so that you stop stressing about things to do. The notes will be there when your praying is done.) Such promptings are the guidance of the Spirit, and they are the doorway to the next step: having resolved to do what you can and ought to do, leave all the rest in God's hands. Resign and deliberately lay down the effort to make everything come out right. Do what is your part, and place the rest in God's care and keeping. Envision yourself handing all the things you cannot fix over to Jesus, who can do all that is needed, and then leave them there. God will be God; it is enough for you to be a servant.

Finally, you are ready to come to the very center of prayer, where you pour out your own deepest heart to God. Speak here your words of gratitude and praise, of repentance, of grief or doubt, of thanksgiving or need or joy. Nothing is out of bounds, and nothing need be hidden, for God is within you and knows every movement of your heart. Reclaim and dwell in your identity as the beloved of God, who came in the flesh to rescue you and promises never to leave you forsaken. Place yourself and all the activities of your life into this framework. Ask God in trust for the strength you need to turn away from everything that binds and burdens you, from every captivity that turns you aside from living in God's presence and rejoicing to do God's will. Ask for all the gifts you need to be who and what God calls you to be, for all the resources you need to fulfill your calling and be at rest. God is faithful and will do it. Say thank you, and go in peace. (Don't forget to blow out the candle.)

Accountability

I have spoken already of the importance of ministers maintaining personal friendships, spending time with people to whom they are *not* the pastor, not a representative of God or the church but simply known as an individual: a basketball player or a fellow gardener or a member of the high school graduating class from way back when. This is partly to provide ministers with respite from the responsibilities and the scrutiny that come with their role. But it is also to help them maintain the boundaries that belong to that role, which properly limit the extent to which they seek personal support from congregants and the information they share with them about personal issues and challenges. These same reasons also make it vital that ministers preserve time to be nourished by all the gifts of life in a family—as a daughter or son, brother or sister, spouse or parent. All of these are relationships in which we are loved and cherished, needed and appreciated for who we are, and where we bring our own human needs for comfort and intimacy, care and support. Some of these connections are likely with people who share our Christian faith, and we might engage with them in Bible study or devotions and prayer, not as a minister but simply as a fellow believer. Ministers lucky enough to have such opportunities for close fellowship will find they are a great blessing that can offer strong support in their Christian life and in their work as pastors.

But here I want to talk about a very particular Christian discipline that goes beyond these general forms of companionship in faith, one which (like prayer) takes many shapes. It is called by various names and lived out in a variety of practices, but all have key elements in common. The most general term for this practice is "accountability," which applies to any practice in which the individual's work of spiritual introspection and the examination of conscience is shared with at least one other person who serves as a partner or guide. Its roots reach back to practices of the early church found in Scripture, where believers are admonished to "bear one another's burdens, and so fulfil the law of Christ" (Gal. 6:2 RSV) and to "confess [their] sins to one another" (James 5:16). Over many centuries, disciplines of confessing sins and seeking spiritual counsel and restoration have taken various shapes—formal and informal, public and private, depending on the nature and visibility of the conduct confessed and whether it was thought to bring scandal on the name of Christ.[4] Monastic and conventual communities fostered practices, called spiritual friendships, that provided mutual spiritual support and oversight between members—a model that continues in use to the present day.[5] Other communities assigned individual confessors or spiritual directors to guide and aid members as well as outsiders who sought assistance. The churches of the Reformation rejected sacramental confession on the grounds that it lacked sufficient biblical foundation (among other issues). However, many of them retained liturgies of confession, repentance, and reconciliation, both for congregations and for individuals who sought the help of a priest or pastor. And even in Protestant churches that have no special forms for hearing individual confessions, giving moral guidance, or declaring sins forgiven, any long-serving minister will have experience with this aspect of pastoral care for congregants in trouble or perplexity.

Practices of this kind are profoundly helpful to anyone who wishes to deepen spiritual life and grow in discipleship. John Wesley's famous dictum that there is no holiness but social holiness did not mean

---

4. This is a long and complex history, and well beyond the scope of the present, more practical work. For a convenient summary, see Lizette Larson-Miller, "Rites of Reconciliation and Healing in Christian History," in *Oxford Research Encyclopedia of Religion*, Oxford University Press, July 2015, http://religion.oxfordre.com/view /10.1093/acrefore/9780199340378.001.0001/acrefore-9780199340378-e-71.

5. The classic work in this area is a twelfth-century treatise by Aelred of Rievaulx, *Spiritual Friendship*, trans. Lawrence C. Braceland, ed. Marsha L. Dutton (Trappist, KY: Cistercian Publications, 2010). For a modern reflection on the moral and spiritual significance of friendship, see Paul Wadell, *Friendship and the Moral Life* (Notre Dame, IN: University of Notre Dame Press, 1989).

(as it is often misunderstood) that only matters of social ethics are important, nor even that all true holiness is socially transformative (although this comes a little nearer the mark). It meant rather that humans grow in holiness in company with others—or not at all. It reflects his view, based on long pastoral experience, that mutual support and accountability is an essential tool for fostering spiritual growth and transformation of life and for holding temptation at bay.[6]

While some form of accountability may be useful for any Christian, it is indispensable for those who propose to lead and guide the church as ministers. To pastors, who must carry the burdens of others' secrets and sins, accountability offers a kind of rest, a place where they can speak the unvarnished truth about their own struggles, frustrations, and doubts. To caregivers, whose work requires them to remain keenly aware of their own emotions, motives, and vulnerabilities, accountability provides at least one other pair of eyes and another source of insight to warn of subtle corrosions in pastoral identity. And for leaders who are tempted by loneliness or despair from the isolation of their position and the constant demands on their time and emotional energy, a wise and trusted spiritual partner or guide can provide a barrier against self-deception and a bulwark against moral collapse. Along with the practice of personal prayer, the practice of accountability—having a person (or, better yet, persons) with whom one can share everything about one's spiritual state and its challenges—is an irreplaceable source of protection and strength.

The discipline of accountability can take multiple forms, influenced by the history and organization of the various Christian traditions. Eastern Orthodox and Roman Catholic churches have the sacrament of reconciliation, or confession, which often includes some degree of moral and spiritual counsel along with the imposition of penance and the pronouncement of absolution. Orthodox and Catholic

---

6. This was the reason that all who responded to Wesley's message were placed in small groups that met weekly under the leadership of more experienced believers. Their task was "to watch over one another in love" by listening to members' accounts of their spiritual struggles and victories, offering counsel, admonition, and encouragement along with prayer support. See John Wesley, "A Plain Account of the People Called Methodist," in *The Works of John Wesley*, vol. 13, *Doctrinal and Controversial Theses II*, ed. Paul Wesley Chilcote and Kenneth J. Collins (Nashville: Abingdon, 2013).

communities also frequently have priests who will serve as confessors over an extended time to other priests or members of religious orders, hearing their confessions and offering ongoing spiritual guidance and oversight. These and other liturgically oriented traditions (Anglican, Episcopalian) may also have people who are specifically trained to serve as spiritual directors, who offer continuing guidance and help to both clergy and laypersons. Protestant communions, which focus more on ministries of Word and preaching and on the ministry of the laity, often have models of accountability based on prayer partnerships or discipleship groups: two or more people who meet together regularly and whose relationship may grow to include deep and candid mutual sharing and oversight.

The basic requirements for effective spiritual accountability are the same as those for personal prayer. Accountability must be regular enough to serve as a reliable source of support, advice, and correction. It must be extended enough to penetrate the facade that pastors are so practiced at maintaining ("I'm fine; how are you?"). And before and after everything else, it must be honest. In fact, it must be most scrupulously honest at the very point when the truth is hardest to share and to hear. The test of whether a practice of accountability can serve and protect those who turn to it is whether they will show up when they would much rather hide, speak when they would rather be silent, and give a searching and unsparing account of what they see in themselves (and in one another) every time.

The practice of accountability can at times be painfully difficult, for it can be a scalding experience to tell the whole truth to other people whose opinion one values and whose respect one would like to keep. But even a word of warning or reproach can be a life-giving and transformative incarnation of grace, making present in the Christian sister or brother God's loving determination to see each of us safely home. Like the deep joy of prayer that can sustain us through grief, accountability is a gift that can only be experienced by those who risk the trial. And since so much is at stake, to be a spiritual friend or guide is a profound and serious engagement with the life and soul of another human. It is not a practice to be entered into lightly, for it represents a substantial commitment in time and availability as well as a willingness to walk with someone through darkness as well as light.

For pastors, at least one of the partners to whom they turn for insight, counsel, and oversight should be someone who shares and understands the particular demands and risks of ministry. Such a person will be readier to recognize the signs of corrosion or distortion in the pastoral role for what they are (perhaps before the pastor does), and better prepared to help take the necessary steps to reestablish boundaries or rechannel personal needs in appropriate ways. However, the ability to offer such help depends on the pastor's attentiveness to her or his own behavior and emotional state, and on careful and truthful self-reporting. Clearly this relationship requires profound trust, not only in someone's willingness to keep confidences but also in his or her wisdom, insight, and spiritual maturity. If the accountability partner is a spiritual director the pastor has contacted through a church or another center of ministry, the pastor's trust can initially only be based on confidence in the certifying agency and the training this spiritual director has received. If this relationship is entered into through an existing connection with a Christian friend of long standing or with a well-known colleague from some other setting, the pastor has somewhat more to build on. But even in the latter case, this new kind of relationship will take time to develop the trust and insight that give it moral authority and effectiveness.

Although I have included models of accountability, such as spiritual direction, in which one person provides oversight to the pastor and the relationship is not mutual, there are particular benefits to practices that are reciprocal. This is especially the case when they involve more than two people. We see others based on who they are but also based on who we are, and our perspective and personal experience color our judgment. When sharing is mutual, participants have an opportunity to gain insight into the person who is offering counsel, and if three or more people are involved, they also receive the benefit of more than one other point of view. This can be helpful when the truth is ambiguous and there are elements of uncertainty. It is also of great help when the truth is clear enough but the pastor is not necessarily ready to recognize it. If two or three people who know the pastor well and who have demonstrated their commitment to her or his welfare agree that there is trouble, a need to change course, or simply a need to take more time for rest and play, it is much harder for the pastor to discount that message. And it is comforting to remember Jesus's assurance: "Where two or three are gathered in my name, I am there among them" (Matt. 18:20). For pastors, who are never quite members of the communities they shepherd, accountability partnerships can be one of their most profound experiences of the body of Christ.

As with prayer, probably the biggest challenge to maintaining a discipline of spiritual accountability is practical: preserving the time it takes and doing so over an extended period of one's life. When this time is to be shared between more than two people, as I have recommended, the logistical problems may be daunting indeed. Commitment, patience, and some flexibility are required. All this is further complicated by our increasing geographic mobility, so that the delicate work of establishing a working relationship with a director, a spiritual friend, or an accountability group can be suddenly disrupted by the news that one is moving a thousand miles away. This can be a real blow and may leave the feeling that one must start all over again, so that pastors in these relationships can lose heart and be tempted to give it up. They must resist the impulse to do so. Pastors who have been working with a spiritual director can get a recommendation from him or her for someone with whom to continue. Those who have a single accountability partner with whom they have met over an extended period may find it better to set up a weekly phone conversation or video chat with that person than to let the practice lapse. While there are aspects of face-to-face encounter that nothing can replace, pastors in these situations may be surprised to find how nourishing and effective even a mediated conversation can be. And if they have been part of a small group practice, those who remain in one location can continue to meet, and their chief care must be to find a way to include the one who must leave, at least until she or he finds an alternative partner or community.

Whatever structure is put in place, part of its purpose is to give pastors the occasion for a careful examination of their own conscience and to help them see their own spiritual condition more clearly and reliably through the eyes of others. It is in that way a means of making all the guidelines and warnings of the preceding chapters more effective in helping pastors remain faithful. But beyond the gifts of insight that the spiritual discipline of accountability offers, it provides something vital that pastors often forget they need. It allows them to hear someone else pronounce over them the double message of the gospel: the severe judgment of God on all that infects and afflicts the creatures God loves, and God's sure mercy on all who turn to God for healing. This is an office that all of us, clergy as well as lay, require others to perform on our behalf. We are creatures of spirit and body, and we need the word as it is embodied in one another, signs of the one Word made flesh in Jesus Christ.

Further Reading

Bonhoeffer, Dietrich. *Life Together*. New York: Harper & Row, 1954.

A classic work on Christian community. Its clear-eyed look at the challenges of a community created not by choice but by the work of God can forestall romanticism and resultant disillusionment about life in Christian communities.

Bush, Joseph E. *Gentle Shepherding: Pastoral Ethics and Leadership*. St. Louis: Chalice, 2006.

An approach to the ethics of pastoral leadership based on professional ethics, unusually attentive to culture and social context in the dynamics of power.

Farley, Margaret. *Personal Commitments: Beginning, Keeping, Changing*. Revised ed. New York: Maryknoll, 2013.

A profound and illuminating look at how commitments give life to our loves while also challenging them. Offers a way forward for those at risk of burnout in ministry.

Fortune, Marie M. *Is Nothing Sacred? When Sex Invades the Pastoral Relationship*. San Francisco: Harper and Row, 1989.

A seminal study of the prevalence, patterns, and effects of clergy sexual misconduct.

Fortune, Marie M., and James Poling. *Sexual Abuse by Clergy: A Crisis for the Church*. Eugene, OR: Wipf and Stock, 2008 [1994].

This follow-up study to *Is Nothing Sacred?* investigates more deeply the dynamics and theological ramifications of clergy sexual misconduct using fictionalized cases and stories from practice and underscoring how relationships go awry and what is at stake for individuals and congregations.

Grenz, Stanley J., and Roy D. Bell. *Betrayal of Trust: Confronting and Preventing Clergy Sexual Misconduct.* 2nd ed. Grand Rapids: Baker Books, 2001.

Drawing on the research done since the scandals of the 1980s and 1990s became widely known, this volume is a good introduction to the topic of clergy sexual abuse, useful to pastors especially for its chapter on prevention.

Gula, Richard M. *Ethics in Pastoral Ministry.* New York: Paulist Press, 1996.

Recommended for its appropriation of historical professional ethics as grounded in basic moral commitments and for its practical advice about recognizing and managing attraction within a pastor-congregant relationship.

Jones, Kirk B. *Rest within the Storm: Self-Care Strategies for Clergy and Other Caregivers.* Valley Forge, PA: Judson, 2001.

A practical guide for clergy who are tempted to over-performance and exhaustion.

Peterson, Marilyn R. *At Personal Risk: Boundary Violations in Professional Client Relationships.* New York: Norton, 1992.

An insightful study of how personal and professional distinctions become muddied and the risks that accompany such confusions. Uses a model based on psychotherapy that is not fully applicable to ministry but is recommended for its subtle and acute analysis that remains illuminating for clergy.

Trull, Joe E., and James E. Carter. *Ministerial Ethics: Moral Formation for Church Leaders.* Grand Rapids: Baker Academic, 2004.

Chapters are framed as a series of questions regarding alternative understandings of the practice of ministry. As its title suggests, it is aimed at intellectual and moral formation of those in training and includes an extensive discussion of the possible role of codes of ethics as well as several examples in current use.

Index

Printed in Great Britain
by Amazon